T0193936

CONSCIOUSNESS:
The Ultimate Reality

Ravi K. Puri, Ph.D.

authorHOUSE®

AuthorHouse™
1663 Liberty Drive
Bloomington, IN 47403
www.authorhouse.com
Phone: 1 (800) 839-8640

Published by AuthorHouse 11/13/2017

ISBN: 978-1-5462-1380-2 (sc)
ISBN: 978-1-5462-1381-9 (hc)
ISBN: 978-1-5462-1379-6 (e)

Library of Congress Control Number: 2017916120

Print information available on the last page.

Dedication

To my parents, for teaching true values of life comprising discipline, morals, and ethics. To Professor O.P. Sehgal, who guided and strengthened my belief in spirituality during my teens.

— Ravi K. Puri

"The whole universal consciousness created the individual consciousness of each of us, experiencing itself from different perspectives, in which each of us create the life we experience."
— *Unknown*

About the Author

Dr. Ravi K. Puri is Ph.D. in pharmacy and has served his profession for almost thirty years in teaching and research. Dr. Puri has a broad range of experience and excelled in the field of pharmacy, biochemistry, and environmental sciences. He has taught and conducted research at the University of Mississippi, Oxford, Oregon State University, Corvallis, University of Florida, Gainesville, University of Missouri, Columbia, and Panjab University, Chandigarh, India. He has published nearly a hundred research papers and scientific reviews in journals of international repute including chapters in reference books published by CRC Press and Lewis publishers. He has been on the review panel of many prestigious scientific journals in the USA and abroad.

He is a celebrated author of a book entitled *Natural Aphrodisiac: Myth or Reality*. The book is widely acclaimed by pharmacists, nurses, physicians, chemists, and herbalists. It is one of the most comprehensive compilations on Natural Aphrodisiacs.

The present publication reveals another aspect of his life about self-analysis and belief in spirituality which he has been practicing for forty years. This experience is being shared with people who are interested in this field and are inquisitive to find out certain aspects of consciousness.

Contents

List of Figures

Foreword

I am but a lowly student of Consciousness, possibly aware of only the small "me." In Dr. Puri's book, however, I have found enough expansive and lucid definitions, examples, and explanations of consciousness to allow me a lifetime of meditation upon them.

As with any student, what we learn, how we learn, and how well we learn, depends largely on what works for us as individual students. In one place Dr. Puri forms the analogy of "senses" to "horses."

Dr. Puri states the charioteer is the determining power for all the good or bad things done or received. He must be careful the horses do not drag the chariot down into the ditch. He must be strong enough to keep control, to manage the horses. He must know the right path and be able to manage the horses on a tough path, so there will be no suffering or sorrow. The reins are the mind. If the driver doesn't have a strong mind, he will have no control over the senses. If he maintains a strong mind, he will be able to use his intellect and understanding, and he will achieve the right power of determination to circumvent problems wherever he goes.

Such a concise analogy allowed me to see clearly the information Dr. Puri was teaching. This volume has been an insightful journey into the "I".

It is to be hoped others who read this tome are led to the proper paths for their continuing education into Consciousness so they, too, are able to learn it is the Ultimate Truth.

Judith A. Stock
Student of the "I"
Poet / Editor / Publisher
Boonville, MO

Preface

I am neither a mystic, nor a preacher of any religion. So, I am not going to suggest you, the path of self-realization, Moksha or Nirvana (freedom from the cycle of birth and death). The purpose of writing this book is about the self-inquiries *such as Who am I? What is the source of my being? Who am I before I am born? What I would be after I die? Who is the seeker, thinker, knower and dreamer? What is consciousness? What does it do? Is it a reality or Myth? Can we evolve without consciousness?*

These questions have been nibbling at me since my adolescence and there were some doubts in my mind about the existence and concept of consciousness and some inherited beliefs or dogmas which had been haunting me all these years. After searching for at least 40 years, I sum up some of my understandings and doubts about the self-inquiries in the shape of this book. I also tried to explain consciousness in a very simple way, though it is a very complex and deep subject. I do hope that it may help some people who are sailing in the same boat and are searching for some answers.

While finishing the book, my latent quest for self-inquiry is not over, but still going on and my expression in the book is not the conclusion of the ultimate reality either. What is going to be the conclusion of ultimate reality, I do not know, and I think nobody ever knew or is going to find out either. Reality about consciousness ('I') is unknown. Most of the explanations by mystics or spiritualists on reality are philosophical and have no scientific proofs or any support. Their explanations are hypothetical. Is 'I' a myth or reality? On the other hand, science has been trying to investigate it but could not come to any decision. It is still a riddle. Understanding of consciousness ('I'), why and how it is evolved, is perhaps the greatest mystery known to science.

Most of the scientists, physicists, biologists, and neuroscientists know nothing about their true selves. How can they inform us about our true selves? In fact, some of them even deny the very existence of the true self- consciousness, commonly known as soul or Atman. However, German physicist and Nobel Laureate Max Planck thought otherwise: "Science cannot solve the ultimate mystery of nature. And that is because, in the last analysis, we ourselves are a part of the mystery that we are trying to solve."

It is also very well stated by a great physicist and Nobel Laureate Erwin Schrodinger "Whence come 'I' and whither go 'I'? That is the great unfathomable question. Science has no answer to it."

Likewise, one of the sacred books on Hinduism, Bhagavad Gita reveals that "Unreal never exists. The real never ceases to exist. The seers of truth have seen (known) the truth of both these" (Bhagavad Gita, chapter 2, shloka 16).

— Ravi K. Puri, Ph.D.
Columbia, MO, 65203
USA

"Lead me from the unreal to real
Lead me from darkness to light,
Lead me from mortality to immortality"
                              —The Rigveda

Acknowledgements

First of all, I am extremely grateful to my consciousness who is the real author of this book. I sincerely offer my humble gratitude from the core of my heart to *That Existence* who gave me the strength and intellect to express my feelings. I could sense *that invisible knower* directing, assisting and protecting me during the various walks of my life. I am honestly indebted to 'That'.

I am obliged to late Siri Govindananda Bharti, known as the Shivpuri Baba, whose teachings inspired me during my youth and I have been following them until today.

I am equally grateful to Brijendra Robert William Eaton of Transformation Meditation Online Institute. His course, Essence of Patanjali Sutra was an eye-opener for me which helped me to comprehend the concept of Consciousness. Though, I never got the opportunity of meeting him, but exchange of some emails was enough for me.

My sincere gratitude to my family and friends for their support. Special thanks to Judith Stock for writing the foreword and Elizabeth Davis for editing the manuscript.

> *"He who sparkles in your eyes, who lights the heavens and hides in the souls of all creatures is God, your Self."*
> — *Siva Yogaswami*

Chapter One:

Introduction: Know Thyself

"Man know thyself: then thou shalt know the universe and God."
— *Pythagoras*

We are living in the age of high technology, and life is also moving at an ultra-pace. Man has gone to the moon and now exploring Mars and other planets. Distance among the planets has been overcome. Communication has become easy and rapid through cell phones, high speed internet, and artificial intelligence. Despite the dramatic advances in high technology medicine such as gene therapy, laser, and plastic surgery, anti-aging devices, high resolution body scanning and scientific miracles like vital organ transplantation; it is amazing that human beings know very little about their true-selves. We have enough knowledge of the various objects and have made tremendous progress in high tech, artificial intelligence, and trying hard to explore the universe. We have also achieved success in these areas to a great extent, and even enhanced life expectancy by prolonging the aging process.

On the other hand, the advancement in technology has resulted in a rat race of developing superior nuclear weapons throughout the world. Every country, big or small, rich or poor, wants to be ahead in this race. All over the world, intolerance, crime, corruption and terrorism are flourishing, and many nations feel insecure among the others. In reality, we are capturing the outer world at the cost of the inner world. It is very pertinent to maintain balance between the outer and inner worlds to establish peace.

It is not out of the way to cite Terrence McKenna, an American ethnobotanist, mystic and author, "We have been to the moon, we have charted the depths of the ocean and heart of the atom, but we have a fear of looking inward to ourselves because we sense that is where all the contradictions flow together."

We need to focus inward to seek the knowledge of the subject ('I') or the seeker. If the knower does not know himself or remains in the dark, then the entire field of knowledge is baseless and unfulfilling. The progress has been made only in the field of objects but the field of subject remained out of knowledge. Hence self-realization of the 'I' is very pertinent and also fundamental part of life. If you know your real-self, you can know the universe and the Almighty. Know thyself and you will know not only the world but the universe, too. There is an old saying — the highest wisdom in life is to *know thyself.* The knowledge of our true-self is the highest wisdom. By knowing one's self, one can realize the true nature of the universe, the true nature of God, and the true nature of everything. Moreover, 'self' is the deity of the body temple. The alchemy of happiness is to transfer the essence of being human from baseness to purity through increasing knowledge of God. Before pursuing God, it is essential to know thyself. A great Indian mystic Nisargadatta Maharaj said, "You cannot transcend what you do not know; to go beyond yourself, you must know yourself."

We ignore 'self' all the time and run around in the temples, churches and mosques to search for God outside, but never worship the soul or true self residing in ourselves which is the part and parcel of our lives. We are carrying the power of eternity within ourselves. Why are we looking outside like a deer that is running around desperately in the woods in search of the smell coming out of his own musk gland located in musk pouch between the genitals and the navel. He thinks the smell is coming from outside while it is coming from within. Similarly, we have poor self-images. We do not know our potentialities. Bliss is within, not without. Jesus Christ put it as, "The Kingdom of God is within you" (Luke 17:21).

Inside us, there is something that has no name. That something is our real identity and knows the real truth. We can't ignore 'that.' Very well-articulated by Banani Ray, an Indian mystic and spiritual guide, "You do not need to go to any temple or church to worship God. The whole existence is God's temple. Your own body is the temple of God. Your own heart is the shrine. You do not need to subscribe to any religion to experience God. The only religion you need to experience God is love, kindness and respect to all beings."

Maharishi Raman, a well-known Indian mystic and sage, eloquently said, "Happiness is your nature. It is not wrong to desire it. What is wrong is seeking it outside, when it is inside."

Carl Jung, Swiss psychologist and psychiatrist, founder of analytic psychology, said, "One who looks outside, dreams, and one who looks inside, awakes." We have a tendency of looking into the outer world instead of looking into the inner world. That's why we dream most of the time.

When we go inward, the first question arises in the mind, *who am I?* This question has vexed many generations since the antiquity and probably would remain unanswered in future, too. This question has sent poets to the blank page, philosophers to imagination, and seekers to the oracle.

According to Erwin Schrodinger, a well-known Austrian physicist, and Nobel Laureate, "The feeling of 'I' is feeling of consciousness itself. You are consciousness. What is this 'I'? You on close introspection, find that what you really mean by 'I' is the ground-stuff upon which all experiences and memories are collected."

3

As per Rene Descartes, French philosopher, mathematician and scientist, "Existence of 'I' is unquestionable. What I am then, I am a thinking and living object. If I stop thinking, I do not exist." Thinking takes place as a form and it must have existence to take a form. He indicates that consciousness is only aware of itself when it takes up form. He made a mistake here. He personified thinking as Existence. It is not thought that produces awareness. It is the awareness that produces thought. Descartes stopped inquiry at the level of thinking where Buddha went deeper and penetrated beyond the deepest level of mind and form. However, the eastern mystics think that consciousness is beyond form and thinking. It is omnipresent and form derives from it. Without consciousness, there would be nothing to experience in any form. How can a form which has a beginning and an end create formless almighty without any beginning and end? Consciousness is metaphysical and may be defined as 'Is-ness' I'm-ness, consciousness, and 'Being-ness'.

Maharishi Raman explained the 'I' as follows: "If you hold this feeling of 'I' long enough and strongly enough, the false 'I' will vanish leaving only the unbroken awareness of the real, immanent 'I', consciousness itself." However, you must get rid of your false identity and all attachments to realize the presence of 'I'.

Max Planck, German physicist and Nobel Laureate, considered consciousness as fundamental and said, "I regard matter as derivative from consciousness. We cannot get behind consciousness. Everything that we talk about, everything we regard as existing, postulates consciousness."

Thus, the answer of *who am I* is: "I am thoughtless pure consciousness." A constant flow of energy in every living being. So, know yourself, sit with yourself and understand yourself. Everything you need, your strength, weakness, courage, fear, compassion, cruelty, love, and hate all exist within you. All emotions of worry, contention, guilt, and compunction come from within. You have the choice as to which you need to find and bring out into the world. If you are constantly seeking outside yourself for approval and validation from others, you can never be happy. Happiness is within. Your whole life, you have been trying to prove to your parents, teachers, friends, relatives, spouses, and so on and on. Your opinion, your way of life, ends up depending on how you are being judged by your social circle. How long can you go on proving yourself to others? There is no end to it. You have to draw a line somewhere. You can't find peace beyond self. You must seek inside. Inner-self is the voice of consciousness which guides self towards the path of its essence. Kabir, a 15th century Indian mystic and saint revered by Hindus, Muslims and Sikhs stated, "If you want the truth, I'll tell you the truth. Listen to the secret sound, the real sound, which is inside you."

You do not know your potential. You are the *beingness* or existence which creates the entire universe. The state of *beingness* is very quiet and devoid of thoughts. There is just silence, nothingness — *'Neti, Neti'* Sanskrit expression meaning, not this, not that. Enjoy the silence to explore thyself. When the thinking mind is still, you see reality, a pure consciousness flowing through everything, living and non-living. You are not only the collection of thoughts, because behind the thoughts is the one who is witnessing the thoughts. That is pure consciousness. A quiet mind is required to realize the unknown. In that stillness, the inner world wakes up and leads to self-realization. When an individual is devoid of all the thoughts and images, he is established in his true nature or true self. When the mind emanates from the self, the world appears and when the self appears or shines, the world disappears.

The thoughts are our universe and we remained engrossed in them all the time, sometimes in the past and sometime in the future. We do not get a moment to know ourselves. Likewise, the bottom of a lake is invisible due to ripples. It is only possible to see the bottom when ripples are diminished and the water is calm. If the water is muddy and disturbed all the time, the bottom remains invisible. If it is calm, clear and devoid of ripples, the bottom is visible. So, the bottom of the lake is our true self, the lake is our mind and the ripples are our thoughts. Thus, with the calm mind, we see our true nature.

To attain stillness of the mind one must live in the present. The mind is a whirlpool of the past and the future and keeps us busy between the two. These are not real either. One is gone and the other has not come yet. Both are in thoughts or imagination. Everything is happening in the **now** which is real. There is no past, no future, only the present moment. The Past is painful memories whether it is good or bad. If good, you are going to miss them. Future is a fantasy, nobody knows about it. It is not real, just an imagination. Hence, there is no need to dwell in the past or dream about the future. The Next moment in your life is not more important than the moment right now. Holding the idea that you can control the outcome of your future life is an illusion that you have created by yourself. You can make efforts to achieve your goals but the results are not in your hands. One can change his destiny but not his fate.

As it is mentioned in Bhagavad Gita India's best-known scripture "You have the right to perform your prescribed duties but you are not entitled to the fruits of your actions. Also, never consider yourself the cause of the results of your activities, and never be attached to not doing your duties." (Bhagavad Gita Chapter 2, text 47). One who does not desire the fruits of his activities is free from all dualities, easily overcome material bondage, and is completely liberated. One should not take the credit or discredit of his actions either. Perform your actions according to your best judgement with honesty and abide in your true self which is our eternal and supreme self.

When you don't know yourself, who you are and what you want, you just become a product of the environment like a rolling stone who gathers no moss. Aldous Huxley, a British writer and social activist said, "If most of us remain ignorant of ourselves, it is because self-knowledge is painful and we prefer the pleasure of illusion." Thus, it is very pertinent to do the self-analysis and to know first thyself and then you will be able to understand the connection with the Almighty. When one wins the mind, he wins the entire world since mind is over the matter. He can never attain peace in the outer world until he makes peace within himself that can be achieved by controlling one's internal and external nature. One must be honest to himself and there should be harmony in his thoughts, talks, and actions. This leads to a rise in consciousness and awareness and finally introduces him to his true self, a higher state of being, based on truth, self-knowledge, and unconditional love.

Amit Ray, an Indian author and spiritual master said, "When you know the knower within, you don't need to know further. When you know the meditator within, you don't need to meditate further. When you truly know the worshiper in you, you are to be worshipped."

> *"The greatest tool of self-love is self-awareness. Once you truly know yourself, love is the only option."*
>
> — *Vironika Tugaleval*

Chapter Two:

'I' is Consciousness

"The 'I' of the self is the eye of the God witnessing and unfolding of creation as Now."

— David Hawking: "The Eye of the I."

The word 'I' is commonly referred to that invisible being who lives in our mind, and who is known only to ourselves. When we refer to 'our' body, it is again a feeling of that invisible 'I'. It is very difficult to separate these two clearly distinct aspects of our being. Whether they are called Spirit and Matter, Mind and Body, or Soul and Body, these two aspects, which are considered as our personal identity, have been examined and discussed throughout history since time immemorial from the perspective of religion, philosophy, science, and mysticism.

Words can only describe a known form. Unknown does not have a form and cannot be perceived and revealed. If you ask somebody, *"Who are you?"* You get the reply immediately, *"I am so and so."* The person will answer his or her name, "I am Dan Crosby," and show you his business card. This name is one's worldly identity but not the real spiritual identity. Your outward physical identity is not yourself. This is the identity given by your parents at the time of your birth. In fact, later, when you grow up, you may not like that name, too. So, what is your real identity? The inquiry baffled and embarrassed people when they couldn't answer. People start thinking on the query of "who am I?" They have nothing to say. Most of them do not know what to say. Blank faces have been seen. They start revealing their limited 'I', but cannot describe limitless 'I' which has no form though a part of them. It is the soul, *the true self.*

Buddha replied on the question of *"who are you?* I am awake." He realized his real identity as true self.

Nisargadatta, an Indian Guru of non-dualism, replied on the question of *who are you?* "You are asking me, who am I? You are not going to get the answer, because one who will get the answer is false. You may have an idea, a concept; you can never see yourself."

The first thought which comes to the mind is 'I'. *I did this. I did that.* Sounds like ego. Is it 'ego'? Yes, it is. Ego is changing and varies from time to time, but 'I' does not change. Knowing *whom am I* results in loss of ego. If you identify 'I' with your real self, it is not ego anymore. However, the feeling of 'I' remains the same from childhood to old age and up to the end. It is a continuing flow of energy. It remains the same, unchangeable and nondestructive. It never grows old with age. This source of energy is neither created nor destroyed. This is an eternal and infinite bliss called consciousness. It is important to realize that you are a pure soul or pure consciousness, nothing else. You are a drop of endless ocean of consciousness. You are limitless. You continually experience yourself as a simple consciousness being, one transcending all experiences. You do not see yourself as limitless 'I' because you have identified yourself with your limited self or your body which is an illusion.

You always say, "This is my hand, my eyes, my heart, my mind, my brain, my car, my sister, my brother, my wife, my son and so on." You identify yourself with others, with your body, mind, and ego. It is a wrong concept. Then what is your identity? Though it has been explained by some mystics of western and eastern philosophy that 'I' is as awareness or consciousness or Atman (soul), the question arises, then who is 'My'? That means 'I' or 'My' is separated from the objects. 'I' or 'My' is separated from the body or mind. Then who is 'I' or 'My'? 'I' and 'My' are always separated. They have distinctive characteristics.

All comprising objects pertaining to 'My' become modified consciousness. 'I' is independent form, whereas 'My' is circumstantial form. 'I' is pure consciousness where 'My' is modified consciousness. 'My' is Maya--an illusion. One gets attached to whatever he refers to as 'My'. Thus, 'I' gets attached to 'My' whereas as 'My' cannot attach to 'I'. 'My' is not related to self. Self is an independent identity. It is invisible and has no locality. 'My' and 'I' are the two parallel lines; they run together in life, very difficult to unite. Despite this, you believe they are one. Once the 'My' is separated from 'I', self-realization occurs. One must drop off all the 'My' belongings from the 'I' which leads to non-attachment. The real 'I' has no possession. Even your body is not yours. Finally, 'I' leaves the body too. When all the 'my' are dumped, only 'I' is left. You get rid of your ego. That is your real self. Maharishi Raman, illustrated the real self as, "It is that out of which the sense of the personal 'I' arises and into which it will disappear."

'I' refers to, who never sits, never moves, never talks, never thinks, never acts, never controls, but always remains calm and blissful. This is 'Self', the absolute 'I' the God within, nothing else. You are completely independent and are the creator of your own destiny. You are ruled by your own omissions and mistakes. Without them, you are the Supreme power or God. A dangerous statement but true according to philosophy of the Vedas—*Tattva Brahm Asi,* or *Tat Tvam Asi*, 'I' am Brahma. That means 'I' am God.
'Thou art that,' I am 'That.'

Maharishi Raman said "God dwells in you, as you, and you do not have to do anything to be God-realized or self-realized. It is already your true and natural state, just drop all seeking, turn your attention inwards, and sacrifice your ego mind to One Self radiating in the heart of your very being. For this to be your own presently lived experience, self-enquiry meditation is a direct and immediate way." As rivers lose name and shape in the sea, sages lose their name and shape in God. He who has realized Him, seeks no more, the mystery is solved, the ego and desire are vanished, and he is blessed.

Likewise, Vivekananda, an Indian Hindu monk who introduced Indian Vedanta and yoga philosophies to the western world, explained, "Each soul is potentially divine. The goal is to manifest this Divinity within, by controlling nature, external and internal. Do this either by work or worship or psychic control or philosophy–by one or more or all of these —and be free." This means stop searching outside and reveal your true self 'I' by contemplating on your ego-self and controlling your internal and external nature.

Further, we are all connected to that supreme source and thus are one. Are we the same inside? Certainly not, because of our thinking, observations, feelings, behavior, actions, and reactions differ from each other. Our belief system, fear, jealousy, emotional addictions, and false ego-self separate us from each other. Albert Einstein put it in a wonderful way, "A human being is part of the whole, called by us, "Universe"; a part limited in time and space. He experiences himself, his thoughts and feelings as something separated from the rest—a kind of optical delusion of his consciousness. This delusion is a kind of prison for us, restricting us to our personal desires and to affection for a few persons nearest us. Our task must be to free ourselves from this prison by widening our circle of compassion to embrace all living creatures and the whole of nature in its beauty."

In essence, we are pure consciousness, the existence of the universe. The universe exists within each of us. We are unconditional, changeless, formless, calm effulgence, endless consciousness which is beyond time and space.

We are all just like inseparable waves of the endless ocean of consciousness. There is only one consciousness, one force, one unified field of energy flowing through all of us. We need to realize this concept which can be experienced and visualize by practice only. As articulated by Tony Samara, a famous spiritual master, "Within each of us is a light, awake, and encoded in the fibers of our existence. Divine ecstasy is the totality of this marvelous creation experienced in the hearts of humanity"

In view of the above, it is concluded that 'I' is consciousness and each soul is divine. It is very well expressed by Anthon St. Maarten, an international psychic intuitive consultant and destiny coach, "You are one thing only. You are a Divine Being. An all-powerful Creator. You are a Deity in jeans and a t-shirt, and within you dwells the infinite wisdom of the ages and the sacred creative force of all that is, will be, and ever was."

Chapter Three:

Concept of Consciousness

"I do not believe that consciousness is generated by the brain. I believe that the brain is more of a receiver of consciousness."

—*Graham Hancock*

There has been a surge in the study of consciousness during the 21st century by biologists, psychologists, and neuroscientists. Ample information is available in the literature with contradicting statements. Consciousness is a very complex term and difficult to define. In fact, it is an unsolved riddle. Man has been conscious about the enigma of consciousness since he gained conscious. Each age has also described consciousness as per its understanding and progression, but nothing conclusive came out. Though extensive research has been done during recent years, the origin of consciousness is still unknown.

Perception:

Modern concepts and implications of consciousness vary from person to person depending upon the level of their consciousness. Philosophers, mystics, physicians, bio-physicists, biochemists, biologists, psychologists, and neuroscientists perceive and imply consciousness very differently and define as per their own perceptions. Most western philosophers and neurosurgeons believe that consciousness evolved from the living system. Neural activity can give rise to subjective experience.

However, the concept of consciousness in metaphysical form has been conceived by the eastern mystics since time immemorial. They called it as *Atman* or soul or divinity. They understood that life emerged from consciousness. However, it was not easy for the scientists to accept eastern concept, rather they viewed it with skepticism.

Hard Problem:

Understanding the origin, the site of formation and evolution of consciousness, is challenging. It is perhaps the greatest mystery known to science and unknown to mankind. How can a physical brain, made of flesh, neurons, fats, and protein molecules give rise to conscious experiences or ineffable qualia? Qualia is the raw sensations of experience. The indefinable experience of pain, pleasure, smell, assorted colors of the flowers, taste of honey, velvet touch, falling in love, feelings of the sound of music, and fragrance of a flower etc., comprise *qualia.* As per Galileo, an Italian astronomer, physicist, engineer, philosopher, and mathematician, "I think that taste, odors, colors and so on reside in consciousness. Hence, if the living creatures were removed, all these qualities would be annihilated."

Likewise, Erwin Schrodinger, a Nobel Laureate said, "I am very astonished that the scientific picture of the real world around me is deficient. It gives a lot of factual information, puts all our experience in a magnificently consistent order, but it is ghastly silent about all and sundry that is really near to our heart that really matters to us. It cannot tell us a word about red and blue, bitter and sweet, physical pain and physical delight; it knows nothing of beautiful and ugly, good or bad, God and eternity. Science sometimes pretends to answer questions in these domains, but the answers are very often so silly that we are not inclined to take them seriously."

Experience of Qualia vary from person to person and it is subjective. It is very difficult to express the feelings of *qualia.* Thus, consciousness is called the *hard problem.* A term coined in 1994 by David Chalmers. Philosopher and Cognitive Scientist at the New York University, he compared it with *easy problems* which can be solved easily such as behavior, perception, learning, attention, ability to discern objects, and reaction to stimuli. Easy problems are objective and can be solved and explained. Whereas, the hard problem is subjective and objective science cannot define it. Patricia Churchland, Professor of philosophy at the University of California, San Diego, disagreed with the terminology of Chalmers and called it a *hornswoggle problem.* As per her objection, it is not fair to decide in advance which problems will turn out to be the hard ones. Secondly, she felt it is a vague explanation. However, consciousness is considered these days a well-known *hard problem* in philosophy and science, and the term is widely accepted among the scientists and philosophers.

Relation with Brain:

It is very interesting to find out the relationship of brain and consciousness. So far, no one has yet succeeded in bridging the deep gap between inner and outer mind and brain. Mind is subjective whereas brain is objective. How does subjective experience arise from objective brain? How does the immaterial come from the material? Needless to go into the details of scientific investigations on consciousness, ample inconclusive information is available in the literature. Neuroscientists think it is a byproduct of the brain. More recently, it is defined as emergent phenomenon of the brain when billions of neurons are fired and communicate with each other resulting in an unimaginable depth of iterations and permutations that give rise to consciousness or experience. As per Patricia Churchland, "The physical brain and its activities are enough to work independently and there is no need of any additional non-physical mind or soul or spooky stuff of the kind that might, for example, survive the death of the brain."

As per mystics, consciousness is metaphysical. It works through the brain but does not require a brain to exist. It was the consciousness that produced the brain as it created everything else in existence. It is not the product of the brain or anything else but itself the Ultimate Reality. It existed before the appearance of matter, time and space and even before the Big Bang. Though there is no evidence to support this statement because it is beyond the comprehension of human intellect. Most of the researchers left the consciousness as metaphysical or extra added in the living system for the time being. Basically, they reach an impasse.

Definition:

The word *conscious* is derived from the Latin word *Con* meaning together and *Scio* means to know. *To know together.* It comprises the knower and the known. It means: subject and the object. When a person is aware of both, the subject and the object, he is conscious. It may be defined as the experience of being awake and aware of the surroundings. Though the definition points towards duality, yet it is difficult to justify this definition.

Moreover, everything, living or non-living exists in consciousness. Even the denial of consciousness is in consciousness. One who speaks is aware of who is speaking and one who is listening is aware of the listener, both are in consciousness. In a way, we are all connected. Those who see that the consciousness within them is the same consciousness within all beings, achieve peace.

Furthermore, experience of being alive is consciousness. Feeling of 'I' means "I am conscious". Behind the thoughts, there is something witnessing the thought that is pure consciousness. Ability to experience the objects, and the surrounding area, is consciousness. Without consciousness, there is nothing to experience any form. Consciousness is not a thing; it is nothing. Consciousness is the all and the nothing. There is not any comprehensive definition that can define consciousness. Consciousness encompasses all definitions. Anything that is, that possesses the quality of *Is-ness*, is consciousness. You are Consciousness. It is the omnipotent matrix out of which form arises, conscious of action, sense of belief, sense of pain, joy and the surroundings all are in consciousness. True Self is pure consciousness which is indivisible, pure, immortal, and omnipresent. Consciousness is everywhere —upon the right, upon the left, above, below, behind, in front. It encompasses the entire universe. It is present in all the creation. A beautiful waterfall, sunrise, and sunset are the reflections of consciousness rather entire nature. To completely experience anything is to be it. In you, consciousness is a human being. In a flower, consciousness is a flower. In a river, consciousness is a river. In a bird, consciousness is a bird. What consciousness chooses to be, consciousness is. It is not without; it is within. It is your experience of yourself. It is like a mirror which reflects its object without losing its quality. *In essence, consciousness may be defined as a circle with infinite as its radius and center, anywhere and everywhere in the universe.*

Consciousness is further classified. There are absolute consciousness, universal consciousness, and individual consciousness. Absolute consciousness is practically impossible to recognize and considered the consciousness of God which comprises everything— the past, the present, and the future. It resides in all and all reside in it, an infinite ocean of different forms of energy. Various forms of consciousness have been described in chapter seven.

Nature:

'I' is embodiment of light — A pure nature of consciousness. Everything is energy, a constant flow in a wave motion. Matter is also energy in a state of motional vibrations. Different matters vibrate at different frequencies. Everything manifests consciousness from primordial vibrations. What is the nature of energy? Energy is the form of consciousness apparently vibrating. *While energy is a moving form of consciousness, the absolute consciousness itself is calm and ubiquitous.* It is very important to understand this concept.

Louis de Broglie, eminent French physicist and a Nobel Laureate explained consciousness by his Broglie's Equation. C = hf, C stands for consciousness, h is Planck's constant and f for frequency. C is responsible for what we experience as in the **Now,** a quantized or minimum unit of an interaction. The sum of all moments C (consciousness) until the current moment is what shapes our concept of life. This is not a philosophical or theoretical statement but an inherent consequence of all matter and energy being quantized. This formula shows how life and death are abstract constructions of Consciousness in the **Now**.

Experience:

The experience of consciousness is unique, ineffable, and beyond mind —a thought-free state of knowingness. It is subtle, comprehensive and transcendental. Moreover, consciousness experience comprises integration of a wide variety of information and the experience is intricate. It is not possible to cover all the famous mystics, the scientists and the poets who had experienced absolute consciousness. There is an extensive list. Survey of the literature reveals that everyone has a unique experience except the majority of them have seen flooding white light. A few very popular examples of renowned persons who had consciousness experience are given below.

Ramakrishna Paramhansa, an Indian mystic and philosopher of Advaita Vedanta (non-duality), felt a torrent of spiritual light overwhelming his mind and gave him peace. He described it as "The living light to which the earnest devotee is drawn doth not burn. It is like the light coming from a gem, shining yet soft, cool and soothing. It burneth not. It giveth peace and joy."

Likewise, Buddha also described his experience as accompanied by *unbounded white light*. Mohammed is said to have languished with 'intolerable splendor' of flood of white light which bestowed upon him, after many days of constant meditation in a cave outside of Mecca. Similarly, when Moses came down Mount Sinai carrying the two stone tablets inscribed with the terms of the covenant, his face shone like the sun, and his clothes became as white as the light.

Paramahansa Yogananda, an Indian Yogi, stated his experience in his very popular book, *Autobiography of a Yogi,* "My ordinary frontal vision was now changed to a vast spherical sight, simultaneously all-perceptive.... A swelling glory within me began to envelop towns, continents, the earth, solar and stellar systems, tenuous nebulae, and floating universes. The entire cosmos, gently luminous, glimmered within the infinitude of my being.... I cognized the center of the empyrean as a point of intuitive perception in my heart. Irradiating splendor issued from my nucleus to every part of the universal structure."

As per David Hawkins, a renowned psychiatrist, physician, and spiritual teacher, the experience of pure consciousness is the cessation of the flow of thoughts replaced by feelings of infinite power, compassion, gentleness, and love. In this state, 'self' becomes the great 'Self'. Hawkins described his own experience about the consciousness in his book, *Power vs Force*. He experienced, "Suffusion of light and a Presence of infinite love, which had no beginning and no end, and which was indistinguishable from my own essence. I became oblivious of the physical body and surroundings as my awareness fused with all-present illuminated state. The mind grew silent; all thoughts stopped. There was inner silence and strength of the presence grew. Personal no more existed and I became the instrument of the infinite Presence. The feelings and scenario of this phase was beyond description."

There is an old saying in eastern philosophy, "When I was there, He was not there, when He was there, I was not there." In essence, when you meet the real self, you forget yourself rather immersed in the Absolute. However, there is not any scientific evidence to support these mystic or consciousness experiences. These symptoms can be due to psychosomatic or hallucinogenic effects or some latent thoughts and belief in the subconscious mind.

Some people even trip on LSD or psychedelics plants for consciousness experiences. Ayahuasca, popularly known as *vine of the soul,* refers to freeing of the soul, is the most powerful consciousness expanding plant that grows in the rain forests of Peru. People go there for *Ayahuasca ceremonies* which are performed under the supervision of Shamans. DMT (Dimethyltryptamine) and serotonin are the main psychedelic constituents besides harmine alkaloids present in the plant. The people who have taken Ayahuasca extract reported extremely altered states of consciousness, access to 'spiritual' realms, and a connection to the Mother Nature which were not possible in normal waking states of consciousness. However, they have also reported some toxic after-effects occurred by its use.

Usually visual hallucination in color occurs with ingesting the decoction of Ayahuasca. Intoxication ends with a deep sleep and dreams. Ralph Abraham, an American mathematician, and Graham Hancock, a British writer and an expert in altered state of consciousness, have narrated their experiences with LSD and Ayahuasca respectively (*U-Tube*). However, it will be interesting to know the difference between an altered state of consciousness with psychedelics and meditation. It is not something new; the use of psychedelic plants known as *Plants of the Gods* have been used in religious ceremonies throughout the world since time immemorial. Richard Schultes and Albert Hofmann have described origins of hallucinogenic use in their book, *Plants of the Gods.* Very interesting description of the origins of hallucinogens, along with some illustration of religion ceremonies, make thought-provoking reading.

Very recently, a new study led by Professor Anil Seth, co-director of the Sackler Centre for Consciousness Science at the University of Sussex, has found evidence that taking psychedelic drugs can induce various levels of consciousness. Brain imaging technology was used to study the effects of LSD, ketamine and psilocybin, the psychedelic compound found in magic mushrooms (Psilocybe species). The neural signal diversity was found higher by these three drugs. As per Anil Seth, "This finding shows that the brain-on-psychedelics behaves very differently from normal. Since this measure has already shown its value as a measure of 'conscious level', we can say that the psychedelic state appears as a higher 'level' of consciousness than normal, but only with respect to this specific mathematical measure."

Rigorous research into psychedelics is gaining importance these days to study the higher state of consciousness. Psychopharmacologists and psychedelic scientists think that use of psychedelics can cure certain depression, anxiety and related mental disorders, and also opens a door to the scientific study of mystical experiences.

Fundamental:

There are two schools of thought about the concept of consciousness. First, consciousness is the fundamental property of matter and is universal. Second, it appears as the emerging result of a complex physical process. The consensus feels it is a fundamental property of the universe and exists metaphysically. Metaphysically, consciousness is an aspect of *Is-ness*, and *being-ness*. Human-ess is only one expression of *being-ness* and in the spiritual world as 'I-am-ness.' Consciousness is the fundamental reality at the basis of all creation. It is very well realized by a famous physicist and Nobel Laureate Erwin Schrodinger, "Consciousness cannot be accounted for in physical terms. For consciousness is absolutely fundamental. It cannot be accounted for in terms of anything else."

Location:

There has been controversy about the location of the soul or consciousness. The Bhagavad Gita, the sacred book of the Hindus, states that the soul is "one hundredth of one hundredth of the width of a human hair". The hair is c.300 molecules wide. The Vedic wisdom points to wave of electrons. Such matter cannot be captured. It cannot be located since it can move freely and promptly throughout our body's electrical field. As per Vedanta, the soul is located at the base of the brain. since this area is the hub of electrical activity. This concept is closer to that of Rene Descartes. The pineal gland, which is in the geometric center of the brain, has been called '*the seat of the soul*' by Descartes. It is directly behind the eyes, hence the biblical saying "The eyes are the windows to the soul" fits very well here. Whether the soul actually resides there or not, is certainly a matter of some debate or needs further investigation.

According to Stuart Hameroff, an anesthesiologist and professor at the University of Arizona, and British mathematical physicist Roger Penrose, consciousness resides in the microtubules of the brain cells which are the primary sites of quantum processing. Upon death, this information is released from the body, meaning consciousness goes along with it. However, there is not any specific site or localization of consciousness. It is here, there, and everywhere in the system comprising outer worlds and inner worlds.

Conclusion:

Despite exhaustive scientific studies carried out on consciousness, there have been some questions which needs further investigations by scientists. What is the origin of consciousness? What is that elemental consciousness with which every brain is born? Is it an illusion or reality? Is it physical or metaphysical? How does it arise? How does it function? Where is it located? Does human consciousness survive death? Can we upload our consciousness to computer? Can we create consciousness?

There are tens of thousands of publications on consciousness. However, there is not any satisfactory proof and explanation for these questions in the literature. Scientists have been struggling to explore these queries but could not reach any conclusive evidence. Nevertheless, so far, they have not been able to do any comprehensive clinical study about the nature of consciousness. Neither could they come up with any device which could investigate and quantify consciousness.

No computer simulation, no matter how sophisticated it replicates a human mind, could ever become conscious. There is more to life than can be explained by scientists and philosophers. Carl Jung, a Swiss psychologist and psychiatrist, remarked, "In each of us there is another whom we do not know."

How can the unknowable be known? That 'unknowable' is changeless, boundless, birthless, deathless, and formless. 'That' has no religion, no belief, no race, no gender, and no sexuality. "That" power holds the worlds in space and would always remain a mystery.

> *"The nature of consciousness is to point beyond itself. It is a tending toward or pointing to... Since consciousness points beyond itself, it is in its very being a self-transcendence."*
> —William Barrett

Chapter Four:

Evolution of Consciousness

"Our greatest human adventure is evolution of consciousness. We are in this life to enlarge the soul, liberate the spirit, and light up the brain."

— Tom Robbins

In view of the discussion in the previous chapter, it is revealed that 'I' is consciousness, a super intelligence, or super natural power that prevails the entire universe. The present chapter deals with the various aspects of evolution of consciousness.

Origin:

Consciousness exists endlessly like an endless infinite ocean of energy. It has been there since time immemorial, even before the Big Bang. There is no beginning and no end. It is immortal, unborn, unchangeable, and self- illuminated, omnipresent, omniscient and omnipotent. Pure consciousness is not an object, cannot be seen or perceived through senses but can be known only when the senses cease their out-of-world orientation. In spite of the extensive research carried out so far, the origin of consciousness is still unknown.

Effect of Stars and Planets:

The age of this physical world travels in repetitive cycles. The Mesopotamian, the Mayan, Aztec, Egyptian, Greek, and Hebrew cultures, all referred to higher times and declining ages. The Greeks called the cycle "The Grand Year". The ancient Indian Vedanta culture called it the "Yuga cycles." Through these ages mankind has repeatedly lost and gained knowledge of the physical laws governing it.

Our stars, planets, and galaxies also influence consciousness through the "Yuga Cycles." *Yuga* is a Sanskrit word which means period or an Era. As per Hindu Vedanta philosophy there are four Yugas:

Golden Age (*Sat Yuga*)
Silver Age (*Treta Yuga*)
Bronze Age (*Dawaper Yuga*)
Iron Age (*Kal Yuga*)

Human consciousness grows and diminishes in cycles. Full Yuga cycle is 24,000 divine years, in which period, the Sun makes a full circle around Sirius, 12,000 years ascending and 12,000 years descending (Figure 1).

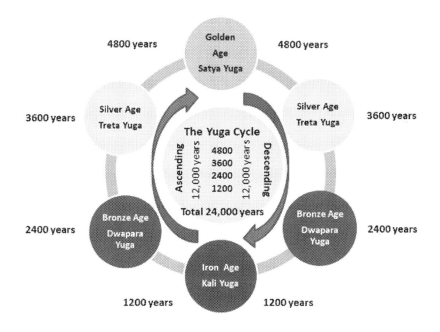

Figure 1: The Yuga Cycle

These four Yuga run in the ratio of 4, 3, 2 and 1. Golden is 4,800 x 360, or 1,728,000 years; Silver, 3,600x360 or 1,296000 years; Bronze, 2,400x360 or 864,000 years; and Iron Age, 1,200x360 or 432,000 years (*Śrīmad Bhāgavatam* 3.11.19). These four Yuga constitute one **Mahayuga** and equal to 4.32 million human years. One year of the demigods is equal to 360 years of the human beings.

During these periods, the position of the planets, stars, and satellite changes and affects the entire cosmos. Sri Yukteswar Giri, an Indian scholar of the Bhagavad Gita and the Bible, explained the "Yuga Cycles" and their effects on the cosmos, in his book, *The Holy Science.*

Consciousness varies in these Yugas (Period). Each Yuga affects the consciousness of mankind. As mankind's consciousness changes, so does civilization and human development. The Yugas not only predict highly advanced ages in the future, but also indicate that they have occurred in the past as well.

Development of human Consciousness is almost 100% in the Golden age. During this period, the world's consciousness is dominated by pure consciousness; golden age as the name suggests, is considered like heaven on the earth. People are very conscientious and have direct intuitive perception and yearning for self-realization. There is hardly any crime. Love, trust, and happiness flow everywhere in the world. The Golden age is also called the 'Age of Enlightenment'.

The Silver age is almost like the Golden Age, the only difference is the godly consciousness is reduced to 75%, and similarly it affects the nature of the civilization of the entire world. In the Bronze Age, godly consciousness is further reduced to 50% and which affects the overall life of the people in the entire world.

In the Iron Age consciousness is reduced to 25%. This is the period full of crimes, corruption, hypocrisy, intolerance, selfishness, intolerance, discrimination, hate, jealousy, and terrorism throughout the entire world. A Majority of people are lacking in self-consciousness, and are more materialistic. They are cut off from nature and do not fear God. The Iron Age is also known as the 'Dark Age.' At present, we are in the Iron Age last descending order and will be followed again by the Bronze Age, in ascending order. Each *Age* is being influenced by the movements of planets and related galaxies.

For years the "Yuga cycles" have been considered as myths, and precession of the Equinox is just a wobbling of Earth's axis. Recently, Walter Cruttendent, a theoretical archaeo-astronomer and author of the binary theory of precession, in his book, *Lost Star of Myth and Time,* shows evidence that the "Yuga Cycles" are not just a fantasy but a reality. This means ancients were right and our views of space and time and the history of civilization would never be the same.

Progression:

Spiritualists believe that consciousness prevails in all living beings as soul or *Atman.* Scientists are now accepting this concept through quantum mechanics.

The degree of consciousness varies from a unicellular organism to multicellular organism depending upon their nature, habitat, environment, and development of the nervous system. The dimension and level of consciousness are also different in these species. The unicellular organism paramecium responds to stimuli. Bacteria are sensitive to heat, light and *pH.* It shows that they have some degree of consciousness called primitive or basic consciousness. The primitive consciousness only recognizes its ecological conditions and survival. Similarly, algae and lower plants eukaryotes also come in this category. It means even on the lower levels of life, there is a profound consciousness or awareness that bonds all things together. Peter Tompkins and Christopher Bird, described in their book, *The Secret Life of Plants*, a captivating interpretation of the physical, emotional, and spiritual relations between plants and man. In essence, the plants may be sentient, despite their lack of a nervous system and a brain.

Slowly we move to advanced consciousness which has a thinking brain. Insects and animals are considered to have advanced consciousness. Insects make their colonies. Reptiles are also sensitive to heat, light, sound and to their surroundings. Birds have some degree of intelligence; they can migrate from one place to another depending upon weather conditions. They make beautiful nests for themselves and even feed their offspring until they are ready to fly. Parrots are known to vocally answer questions and copy some sentences. Pigeons used to take messages tied to their ankles flying miles away from one place to another and delivered the messages to the right place and right person. The author had the experience of sending messages to and fro by pigeons miles away during his teens to confirm this concept. B.F Skinner, a leading 20th century psychologist taught pigeons to play ping-pong at the Harvard Psychology Department in 1950. It is amazing but provides proof of some degree of consciousness in birds, too.

The intelligence of higher animals is well-known. Monkeys, horses, bear, tigers, lions, and related species work very diligently in the circus. Bears can dance; horses can do many tricks where elephant also play with the ball. Tigers and lions perform many things. These metaphors indicate some degree of consciousness is present in animal species.

Animal and human consciousness:

Animals are gregarious, living together, intelligent, sensitive, and emotional but lack discernment. Animals do not have *self-consciousness,* which is peculiar to human beings, and differentiate them from humans. An animal is not able to *know itself.* It has only physical consciousness. It has no self-consciousness. An animal feels discomfort and pain. They experience grief, too. It is not able to analyze its own mental states. A man not only 'knows', but he 'knows that he knows.' This is either mental consciousness or self-consciousness. The man not only 'feels' or 'senses' things, but he has words to express his feelings and sensations. Finally, humans have the ability to see far into the future, whereas animals do not have this instinct. Nevertheless, human beings possess the potential with their highly developed nervous system to raise their consciousness to super-consciousness. Lastly, *reasoning* is found only in human beings. He collects the data, analyzes, concludes and decides.

Expansion:

Expansion of consciousness is the engine behind the train of biological evolution. With the evolution of the living organisms, the degrees of consciousness also change simultaneously according to the changes in their body system. Man's evolution, is an evolution in consciousness. Man is the highest experiment of the evolutionary process. He has the finest nervous system and more developed brain. Consciousness is more developed in human beings and called *Intellectual Consciousness.* As per Hindu Vedanta philosophy, one must change 8.4 million forms before attaining a human's life. Evolution of a man is the evolution of his consciousness. The human form is, up until now, the highest form on this plane of existence. With the attainment of knowledge and understanding of the self, our consciousness is being expanded every day. When the expansion reaches a plateau, it finally immerges into the cosmos or the absolute consciousness just like a river which loses its identity in the ocean.

Levels:

Levels of consciousness vary in living organisms. The living organism experiences through the body and mind so its experience is not the whole, it becomes relative to body condition or mind and subject to change, and thus consciousness is modified. However, the absolute consciousness, or pure consciousness, never changes and remains the same. We have pure consciousness and modified consciousness in the body. Modified consciousness is nothing but the mind comprising of thoughts, memories imaginations, and experiences called Human consciousness. Human consciousness varies in persons and is found at various levels of energy. Their intellects depend upon the *levels of their consciousness.* If a person possesses consciousness equal to a tennis ball, and if he reads a book, his understanding will be equal to the tennis ball size consciousness. If he possesses a high energy level of consciousness, then his understanding after reading that book will be great. So, in other words, an individual's intellect is directly proportional to the level of his consciousness.

David Hawkins, a renowned psychiatrist, physician, and spiritual teacher, came up with numbers of conscious levels from 10-1,000, through his methodology applying Kinesiology technique. Kinesiology is the science of study of the mobility of muscles. Through this technique, he found the intimate connection between mind and body, revealing that the mind thinks with the body itself. With a computer program and mathematical equation through applied kinesiology, he calibrated the various strength level of consciousness of mankind.

According to Hawkins, half of the population of the world falls below the energy level of 200. All dictators of the world also come in that section. People full of hate, greed, anger, lust, guilt, fear also have consciousness level below 200. All levels below 200 are destructive of life both in the individual and society at large. Levels of consciousness are always mixed and are based upon various areas of life in an individual. An individual's overall level is the sum-total effect of these variation levels. Low energy levels of 20-30 are full of shame and guilt. They are very dangerous and caused by sexual abuse. Shame produces neurosis. People are shy, withdrawn, and introvert. It further produces false pride, anger and guilt. Low energy levels of 50 are characterized by apathy, poverty, despair, and hopelessness. Energy levels between 50-75 are the levels of grief, sadness, loss, and dependency. They remain in depression and lamenting on the past. Losers, chronic gamblers, drunkards, drug abusers fall in this category. Energy level of 100 indicates fears of all kinds such as enemies, old age, death, and social fears. Fear of losing someone you love. Fears become obsessive and limits the growth of the personality and leads to inhibition. Energy levels of 125-200 comprises desire, anger, and false pride. Desire for more money and sex is a kind of addiction. Anger leads to self-destruction and false pride leads to arrogance and denial.

Above the energy levels of 200-250 come people of integrity. Fire fighters and some police officers of good moral character are at the conscious level of 300. Above 300-400 levels of consciousness cover celebrated scientists, professors, doctors, surgeons, and engineers. 500 level of consciousness comprises mostly spiritual people. If someone wants to attain higher consciousness level, he must embrace love. Be as loving as you can. Love all. 600-700 levels are for people who live in bliss, *Sat Chit Ananda*. They are fully aware of '*Self*' and are enlightened. Mostly prominent and well-recognized spiritual Gurus have that kind of level.

Hawkins put Avatars like Krishna, Buddha, and Jesus, at the consciousness level of 1000. This is the highest level of consciousness with no further evolution.

Qualities:

Expansion of consciousness imparts many *qualities* in a person. His communication skill is improved by free-flowing thoughts. His Intellect and skills are enhanced. He becomes fearless with strong inner strength and sense of wellbeing. He loses interest in materialistic objects and is more attracted towards nature. His heart is full of love, gratitude, appreciation, and affection for others. There is no jealousy and hatred.

We are all one and connected. Our belief system, fear, ego, desire, and jealousy separates us from each other. With the enhancement of consciousness, we overcome our differences and start realizing the reality. Moreover, our awareness about ourselves and the world around us is so limited that we are ready to destroy ourselves. For the survival of humanity, an evolution of consciousness is very crucial. There is no way to advance spiritually without committing oneself to the happiness and welfare of living beings. Every person has a vast, endless, and timeless love that awaits within each of us to be discovered by those who sincerely seek it.

Some people are in different dimensions and find real joy and beauty which cannot be attained by ordinary humans. The internal bliss and joy depend upon the level of consciousness achieved.

It is articulately expressed by V.S. Ramachandran, a neuroscientist known for his work in the fields of behavioral neurology and visual psychophysics, in his book, *The Tell-Tale Brain: A Neuroscientist's Quest for What Makes Us Human,* "How can a three-pound mass of jelly that you can hold in your palm imagine angels, contemplate the meaning of infinity, and even question its own place in the cosmos? Especially awe inspiring is the fact that any single brain, including yours, is made up of atoms that were forged in the hearts of countless, far-flung stars billions of years ago. These particles drifted for eons and light-years until gravity and change brought them together here, now. These atoms now form a conglomerate— your brain—that can not only ponder the very stars that gave it birth but can also think about its own ability to think and wonder about its own ability to wonder. With the arrival of humans, it has been said, the universe has suddenly become conscious of itself. This, truly, is the greatest mystery of all."

Chapter Five:

Scientific Belief of Consciousness

"The idea that excites me the most concerns the two greatest puzzles in science: the origin of the universe, and the origin of consciousness."

— *Michio Kaku*

Both science and spirituality are pursuing truth. One is searching the outer world whereas the other is searching the inner world. Both have the same goal but their ways and approaches are entirely different. Science is limited to the realm of objective observation. Consciousness is subjective. It is beyond intellect and reasoning. In fact, all intellect and reasoning are part of consciousness. So, science is a part of consciousness. Without being conscious, scientists cannot think. Without consciousness, nothing can be known. How can we solve a problem when we are part of it?

The nature of consciousness has intrigued philosophers and scientists for thousands of years. But can modern neuroscience ever hope to crack this mysterious phenomenon? Consciousness has been the challenging problem for scientists ever since its conception. It has been a riddle for the scientists who could not solve the mystery until today. They desperately want to find the concrete proof of this mystery. Many of them tried to explain it but their explanations were not comprehensive. Survey of the literature indicates that most of the scientists believe in the ultimate truth of consciousness. They could not deny the presence of an unknown intelligent power who created and runs the universe. Some of the examples are given below.

Isaac Newton (1642-1726) an English mathematician, astronomer, and physicist who is widely known for his pioneer work in physics, Newton's Laws, expressed his views about consciousness, "I know not how I seem to others, but to myself I am but a small child wandering upon the vast shores of knowledge, every now and then finding a small bright pebble to content myself with while the vast ocean of undiscovered truth lay before me."

Max Planck (1858-1947) a German Physicists, originator of quantum theory and Nobel Laureate did not believe that consciousness is derived from matter and the brain produces consciousness. On the contrary, he believed that matter is derived from consciousness. He regarded consciousness as fundamental. He perceived, "There is no matter as such. All matter originates and exists only by virtue of a force which brings the particle of an atom to vibration and holds this most minute solar system of the atom together and behind this force the existence of a conscious and intelligent mind. This mind is the matrix of all matter."

Guglielmo Marconi (1874-1937) an Italian electrical engineer known for his pioneer work in long distance radio transmission and shared the 1909 Nobel Prize in Physics, said, "The more I work with the powers of Nature, the more I feel God's benevolence to man; the closer I am to the great truth that everything is dependent on the Eternal Creator and Sustainer; the more I feel that the so-called science I am occupied with, is nothing but an expression of the Supreme Will, which aims at bringing people closer to each other in order to help them better understand themselves."

Werner Karl Heisenberg (1901-1976) a German theoretical physicist and the Nobel Prize winner, said, "Belief in God is a natural result of studying science. The first gulp from the glass of natural sciences will turn you into an atheist, but at the bottom of the glass God is waiting for you."

Carl Sagan (1934-1996) an American astrophysicist stated, "Science is not only compatible with spirituality; it is a profound source of spirituality. When we recognize our place in an immensity of light-years and in the passage of ages, when we grasp the intricacy, beauty, and subtlety of life, then that soaring feeling, that sense of elation and humility combined, is surely spiritual. The notion that science and spirituality are somehow mutually exclusive does a disservice to both." He strongly believed in God, religion and spirituality.

Brian Josephson and William Daniel Phillips, great physicists and Noble Laureates, also believed that the universe was created through the action of an intelligent power.

Nobel Prize winners Erwin Schrödinger and Wolfgang Pauli also held the belief that the universe was created by an intelligent power. Arno Penzias believed that the universe was the result of a supernatural plan whereas Charles Townes, a Nobel Laureate, assumed the existence of God since science could not explain the origin of the universe. Thus, he believed there was a need for some religious or metaphysical explanation. He believed in the concept of God and in His existence.

Richard Errett Smalley (1943-2005) a Nobel Laureat, believed the fine-tuning of the universe was designed and created by God. He stated, "God did create the universe about 13.7 billion years ago, and of necessity has involved Himself with His creation ever since. The purpose of this universe is something that only God knows for sure, but it is increasingly clear to modern science that the universe was exquisitely fine-tuned to enable human life. We are somehow critically involved in His purpose. Our job is to sense that purpose as best we can, love one another, and help Him get that job done."

George David Wald (1906-1997) an American scientist and Nobel Laurate in medicine, believed "Consciousness was not produced by matter and that matter and life existed only because of preexisting consciousness. Mind, rather than being a late development in the evolution of organisms, had existed always; that this is a life-breeding universe because the constant presence of mind made it so. What we recognize as the material universe, the universe of space and time and elementary particles and energies, is then an avatar, the materialization of primal mind."

Arthur Compton (1892-1962) an American physicist and a Nobel Laureate, believed that the "Orderly, unfolding of the universe demonstrated a plan created by God. It is not difficult for me to have this faith, for it is incontrovertible that where there is a plan there is intelligence-an orderly, unfolding universe testifies to the truth of the most majestic statement ever uttered-In the beginning, God."

Nikola Tesla (1856–1943) a Serbian-American inventor, electrical engineer, and physicist, best known for his contributions to the design of the modern alternating current (AC) electricity supply system, not only believed in God but also followed Vedanta like Erwin Schroder. Tesla said, "My brain is only a receiver. In the universe, there is a core from which we obtain knowledge, strength, and inspiration. I have not penetrated into the secrets of the core, but I know that it exists."

Albert Einstein (1879-1955) a famous German American Scientist and Nobel Laureate said, "Natural laws were designed by intelligence, everyone who is seriously involved in the pursuit of science becomes convinced that a Spirit is manifested in the laws of the universe – a Spirit vastly superior to that of man, and one in the face of which we with our modest powers must feel humble. In this way the pursuit of science leads to a religious feeling of a special sort, which is indeed quite different from the religiosity of someone more naive."

Antony Hewish, a British inventor and Nobel Laureate in physicist, said, "I believe in God. It makes no sense to me to assume that the Universe and our existence is just a cosmic accident, that life emerged due to random physical processes in an environment which simply happened to have the right properties."

Kurt Gödel (1906-1978) an Austrian American Logician, mathematician and philosopher, did not believe in materialism, or that the mind was produced by the brain, or that the brain evolved through Darwinian evolution. The brain is a computing machine connected with a spirit. He believed a human was a spirit connected with a physical body and that there were beings higher than humans and other worlds than earth. The world in which we live is not the only one in which we shall live or have lived. There are other worlds and rational beings of a different and higher kind. It is not out of the way to mention Guru Nanak Dev (1469- 1539) a renowned Indian mystic, cited in his version of *Jap Ji Sahib* that there were 18,000 worlds in this universe and some super power runs the universe. It is amazing, how he could imagine the unmanifested universe at that time.

A highly respected scientist, Machio Kaku (1947) an American theoretical physicist and futurist known for his pioneer work on string theory said, "I have concluded that we are in a world made by rules created by an intelligence. Believe me, everything that we call chance today won't make sense any more. To me, it is clear that we exist in a plan which is governed by rules that were created, shaped by a universe intelligence, and not by chance."

There are numerous examples of famous scientists who could not deny the presence of some super natural power balancing and running the universe. Some atheists think that modern science has removed the need for God. However, many of the greatest scientists believe just the opposite, they strongly feel the existence of an intelligent designer of the universe, a kind of super natural power.

Stephen Hawking an English theoretical physicist, and cosmologist, mentioned in his famous book, *The Grand Design,* that quantum theory is the theory of everything. There is no soul, no consciousness, and no free will. The human beings are biochemical robots governed by the brain. There are many conventional physicists and scientists who follow the same belief. One of them, Francis Crick (1916-2004), co-discoverer of DNA, said that awareness is nothing more than a feeling generated in the brain and "You, your joys and sorrows, your memories and your ambitions, your sense of personal identity and free will, are in fact no more than the behavior of a vast assembly of nerve cells and their associated molecules."

Stephen Hawking further elaborated his view by saying, "It is hard to imagine how free will can operate if our behavior is determined by physical law, so it seems that we are no more than biological machines and that free will is just an illusion." It is really astonishing to know the views of these intellectuals about their denial of the soul, free will, or consciousness. They did not know that their intellect and denial both prevail in the consciousness. If the brain is running the entire process then who is running the brain? The brain is like a computer unable to function without the electricity. That electricity is absolute consciousness.

Very recently, scientists claim that quantum theory proves consciousness moves to another universe at death. A book entitled, *Biocentrism: How Life and Consciousness are the keys to Understanding the True Nature of the Universe,* has baffled the scientists. It reveals that life does not end when the body dies, and it can last forever. The author of the book *Robert Lanza* is an eminent scientist and physician who believes in this theory of biocentrism that means life and consciousness are fundamental to the universe. Consciousness creates the material universe, not material creates the consciousness.

More recently scientists at the University of Toronto and Paris Descartes University, say Consciousness Could Be a Side Effect of 'Entropy'. They used a probability theory called statistical mechanics to model the networks of neurons in nine people's brains-including seven who had epilepsy. They were looking at synchronisation of neurons. First, they compared the connectivity patterns when participants were asleep and awake; and then they looked at the difference when five of the epileptic patients were having seizures, and when their brains were in a normal, 'alert' state. In both cases, they saw the same trend — the participants' brains displayed higher entropy when in a fully conscious state. They stated, "We find a surprisingly simple result: normal wakeful states are characterised by the greatest number of possible configurations of interactions between brain networks, representing highest entropy values,"

Thus, the researchers conclude that consciousness could simply be an "emergent property" of a system that's trying to maximise information exchange. However, there are some big limitations to this work—primarily the small sample size. It's not fair to spot any conclusive trends from only nine people, particularly as everyone's brains responded slightly differently to the various states. The research is in a very rudimentary stage and nothing can be concluded.

Conclusion:

Science has not been able to solve the mystery of consciousness until today. They could not come to any decision about its existence as physical or metaphysical. Many scientists who have studied consciousness believe, they are close to solving the puzzle, but they fervently disagree with each other about the solution. A majority of the Nobel Laureate scientists believed in the presence of some unknown force, super intelligence or super power running the universe. However, with the passage of time, scientists are coming closer to mystical vision about consciousness through quantum mechanics.

Recent investigation by Stuart Hammeroff and British physicist Roger Penrose revealed that consciousness resides in the microtubules of the brain cells, which are the primary sites of quantum processing. Upon death, this information is released from the body. They are coming closer to the Vedanta concept about soul leaves the body after death.

Neuroscientists are working on the neural mechanisms of human consciousness at an astonishing pace. Neurobiologists Francis Crick of the Salk Institute for Biological Studies in San Diego and Christof Koch of the California Institute of Technology, suggested that consciousness may arise from certain oscillations in the cerebral cortex, which become synchronized as neurons fire 40 times per second. Crick and Koch believe the phenomenon might explain how different qualities of a single perceived object such as its color and shape, etc. which are processed in different parts of the brain, are merged into a coherent whole. Who knows, one of these days neuroscientists may surprise the world by solving the mystery of consciousness.

Everything is in consciousness. The eminent scientists who are investigating consciousness are also part of consciousness, including their intelligence. How can a fish describe an ocean? It is very well expressed by Albert Einstein, "No problem can be solved from the same level of consciousness that created it."

> *"The key to growth is the introduction of higher dimensions of consciousness into our awareness."*
> — *Lao Tzu*

Chapter Six:

States of Consciousness

"Life is a series of sensations connected to different states of consciousness."
— *Remy de Gourmont*

There are four states of consciousness as per Hindu Vedic philosophy cited by Mandukaya Upanishad. Nisargadatta, a well-known Indian mystic of 20th century, extended it to five states. Maharishi Mahesh Yogi, one of the well-known Indian mystics and founder of Transcendental Meditation, categorized further to seven states of consciousness (Figure 2).

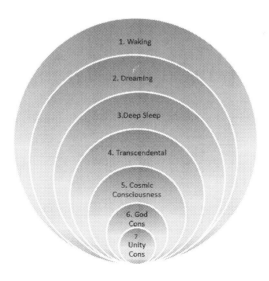

Figure 2: States of Consciousness

According to Vedic literature, the four heads of Brahma (creator of the universe) represent the four states of consciousness (Figure 3). Brahma in Hindu literature represents an endless and infinite consciousness.

**Figure 3: Four heads of Brahma representing
the four states of consciousness.**

1. Waking
2. Dreaming
3. Dreamless
4. Transcendental

It is very important to understand the four states of consciousness. Once you understand the first three states, the fourth one is pertaining to eternal journey. It will lead you to the internal world where all the activities are performed in a subtle manner.

1. Waking:

The first aspect of consciousness is — '*Self*' in the waking state that shines through the senses outwards to the external world.

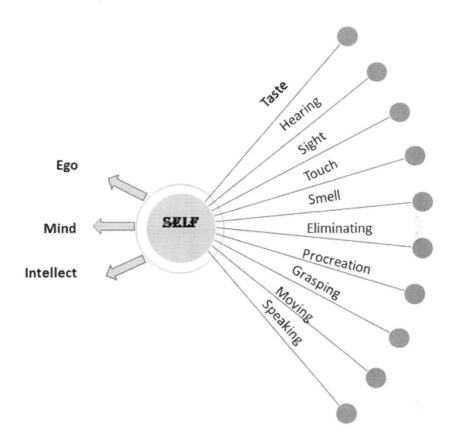

Figure 4: Waking State — Self shines through the senses outwards.

All perceptions are turned outward. It is a physical world. Physical things are seen, heard, and perceived in the conscious mind through its senses. The waking state is physical, emotional, and intellectual and all perceived objects seem to be real. The awakened seeks experience in the present through 13 sources, from these, 10 are senses as shown in Figure 4 (Five organs of sensing— hearing, touching, tasting, smelling, and seeing. Five organs of actions- speaking, handling, walking, generating and excreting, and the other three are mind, intellect, and ego).

In the waking state of consciousness, space and time persist. A person is responsible for the creation of his own world of space and time. Mind, intellect and ego play a significant role in shaping the life span of an individual. If he controls his senses and ego while filtering through the mind and intellect, he can make use of the waking state to create his own world. Intellect is the faculty of discerning between good and bad. If one controls his mind he can be successful. The mind stays in the past or imagines the future. It is restless. It is never free. It is always occupied with objects, thoughts and emotions. It needs filtering through the intellect and time. Time is a great filter and healer. The best way to calm the mind is to stay in the present. Once the mind is free from negative thoughts it can be very useful for self-therapy. Thus, the waking state is a means to expand one's consciousness.

2. Dreaming:

Dreaming is the second state of consciousness. The dreaming stage is also equipped with 13 instruments like in the waking stage as shown in Figure 5.

Dream senses to experience dream objects, a dream mind to feel, a dream intellect to think dream thoughts, and a dream ego to experience the dream life. The self-consciousness is shining through the dreamer. All dreams appear in light, even though the waking senses are inactive and objects are perceived in darkness. The *Self* (consciousness) is shining through the dreamer, just as it shines through the waking stage. Physical, emotional and intellectual objects seems to be real in dreams too. Self-engages the subtle objects of the mental realm. The only difference, physical body is inactive.

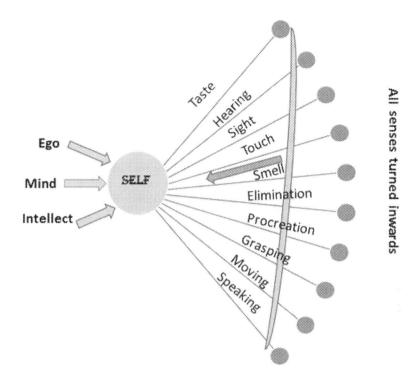

Figure 5: Dreaming Stage—Consciousness turned inward and shines through the dreams.

During the dream phase, consciousness turns into the inner world. It occurs in the unconscious mind. One never loses his identity during this state. Dreamer remains in his own world through dreaming. In this stage, the self illuminates only subtle subjects. All the thoughts, memories and feelings gathered in the waking stage are expressed in pictorial form. Like the waking stage, the dreamer believes his dream world as real. The feelings of fear, anger, frustration, and crying are all real in dreams. The dreams affect the body. The mind enjoys and suffers during dreams. The experience of crying, weeping, sweating and jerking in dreams are the proof. The dream and events in the dream appear to be real during the time of the dream. In fact, dreams are the result of unfulfilled desires, wishes, wants, fears, conflicts restrictions, and hesitations one faces in his life from time to time. These are stored in the subconscious mind. When the conscious mind relaxes, these appear in the dreams. That is what creates dreams.

Sometimes one perceives in the dreams, events and places which have no connection in his present life. All the diverse types of experiences in dreams are the result of impressions and memories of actual experiences obtained at different times, places, ages and births.

As per the Upanishad, "In the dream state, mind experiences greatness. Whatever was seen, it sees again, whatever was heard, it hears again, whatever was perceived at various places, it experiences again and again. It perceives all by becoming all that was seen or not seen, heard or not heard, perceived, or not perceived and whatever is real and unreal." (Prashanopanishad 4.5)

3. Dreamless:

The dreamless state is deep sleep and may be defined as the state, saturated with calmness, where one doesn't desire any external objects, doesn't see any internal objects In the deep sleep state of consciousness, there is no external or internal world and neither desire for any gross or subtle object. There is no awareness of time and space. All such experiences merged into one unified field of consciousness. The person experiences bliss, state of *Sat Chit Ananda means in total bliss.* It occurs in the subconscious mind. However, we do not lose our identity in this case either. In deep sleep, there is no knowledge of anything. It lasts only for a short time generally for about three hours. After that the dreaming stage appears.

Waking state, dreaming state, and dreamless state are being perceived by one's self-conscious entity or *Atman* which never changes but it is always the same knower all the time.

4. Transcendental:

In the transcendental state, consciousness is neither turned inwards nor outward; the mind and the senses are completely silent, but consciousness is fully awake. There is no cognition. No experience of any kind. This is pure consciousness, a real self to be realized. It is serene, tranquil, and blissful. Oneness, nondual, feeling of 'I- ness' and self-illuminates. It is unknown, incomprehensible, undefinable, unthinkable, indescribable, unchanging, and formless. It is the 'Self', the lord of all, creator and dissolver of all. He is not knowable by perception turned inwards or outwards or by combining both. He is neither that which is knowable nor that which is unknowable. He is the sum of that which might be known. He cannot be seen or defined. The only proof of his existence is union with Him. The world appears and disappears in Him.

According to Nisargadatta, "It reveals that 'I' must be beyond that "I am," because I am the knower of that "I am." I am not actually the "I am" but rather THAT which is aware of the "I am." I am pure awareness which is prior to consciousness."

5. Cosmic:

The cosmic state of consciousness is a higher form of consciousness than that possessed by an ordinary man. As the name indicates, consciousness of the cosmos means consciousness of the universe. During this stage, there occurs intellectual enlightenment which places the individual on a new dimension and he feels elevated with joy and a sense of immortality and eternal life. This state of cosmic consciousness is also called witness-consciousness, *illumination, liberation, and the baptism of the Holy Ghost.*

As per Maharishi Mahesh, an Indian sage, seeker, and founder of Transcendental Meditation, "Gradually, with the ability of the nervous system to stay in contact with the fourth state, one develops the ability to sustain that inner silence, which inbounded inner reality simultaneously while one is doing things, thinking thoughts (being) active. Eventually, that becomes stabilized and it becomes a permanent state of consciousness." One goes beyond the small 'me'. The entire world is seen as being transient, transitory, illusory…..this is the first permanent awakening.

6. God Consciousness:

From the fifth state, a very similar progression takes place as one transcends thought and eventually reaches the self, the Atman. According to Maharishi Mahesh, "Initially, our perception is on the surface of things. But because there is this connection with the deepest within, this creates the capacity to see more deeply. As the perception of the outer world becomes deeper and subtler, attention goes to more and more pleasing levels—subtler is more pleasing more unbounded, closer to that pure level where everything is bliss." The heart opens. That's a very powerful force. The heart can overtake anything. Even the noise becomes pleasing. That is God Consciousness.

The person who has risen to cosmic consciousness possesses unlimited love flowing in all directions. The individual in Godly consciousness overflows in love and devotion to God, and is fully transformed. Such a person has a special glow on his face and assertiveness in his speech and actions. Such an individual is in communion with God all the time. He sees the glory of God, hears the music of nature and speaks the words of eternal being.

7. Unity State of Consciousness:

This is the last state of consciousness where there is no duality. Everything leads to non-duality and tranquility. There is only one absolute consciousness. As per Maharishi Mahesh, "This is the full awakening, never ending process. Always keep on unfolding in the way of expansion and deepening." No duality. No difference in real and un-real, the self and non-self, the absolute and the relative, there is only one. In unity consciousness, my-self is the 'self' of all. There is only oneself. Atman is Brahma, the true self. After gaining the higher consciousness, our consciousness becomes universal and absolute.

Love, beauty and Truth are experiences of unity consciousness. Deepak Chopra, an American author and founder of the Chopra Center, eloquently stated, "Unity consciousness is a state of enlightenment where we pierce the mask of illusion which creates separation and fragmentation. Behind the appearance of separation is one unified field of wholeness. Here the seer and the scenery are one."

Chapter Seven:

Various Kinds of Consciousness

"We who have been born Buddhist, Hindu, Christian, Muslim, or any other faith can be very comfortable in each other's temples, mosques, and churches, praying or meditating together to create a spiritual mass of consciousness which can overcome our greed, hatred, and illusions."

— Ari Ariyaratne

There are different kinds of consciousness mentioned in the literature. It is very pertinent to illustrate those terms and their explanation to avoid any confusion. Consciousness is classified as follows.

1. Simple
2. Human
3. Cosmic
4. Collective
5. Absolute

1. Simple:

Simple consciousness is attained by higher animals and by an ordinary human being. By means of this faculty, animals have limited consciousness of their own body and surroundings, where as simple consciousness in humans can be expanded to any higher level through self-consciousness. The main difference, animals do not possess self-consciousness which differentiate them from the human beings.

2. Human:

Human consciousness is above the simple consciousness. It is possessed by mankind, consisting of thoughts, reasons and imaginations. It is also known as self-consciousness. It is the sense of differentiating between right and wrong along with understanding of relationships and their importance in and outside the family. By this faculty, a person is not only conscious of worldly objects but also his own self. Nevertheless, he becomes conscious of himself as a distinct entity apart from the rest of the world. He realizes the universe is not a dead machine but a living presence. An individual existence is continuous beyond death. A sense of well-being only belongs to man. Human consciousness experience depends upon the body, mind, soul, and the surrounding world. Human consciousness is also influenced by many factors such as heredity, environment, and knowledge one gains while growing with the passage of time. It changes with time as the person grows and attains more knowledge and wisdom. Human consciousness through self-realization can possess higher levels of consciousness.

No animal can realize in this way; their consciousness is limited. Animals are not self-conscious. They cannot differentiate even their own family members. Incest in animals is the primary example to support this statement. The people who indulge in incest have animal like consciousness. Human consciousness is further divided into Outer consciousness and Inner consciousness. Outer consciousness means consciousness in which the outer world or objective world is cognizant through our senses. Inner consciousness means consciousness of inner forces, inner perception, towards the soul or *Atman,* nothing else. It is separated from the sense impressions and from external perceptions. Outer consciousness gets attached to materialistic things and ultimately leads to murkiness and cynicism whereas Inner consciousness brings happiness and solace to the mind. *Sat Chit Anand,* absolute happiness.

3. Cosmic

Cosmic consciousness is also known as Universal consciousness. Cosmic consciousness has been recognized from time immemorial in Eastern and Western countries of the world. The majority of the civilized people in these countries even today pay tribute to teachers, Masters or Gurus who possessed the cosmic consciousness. They respect them and follow their teachings. These teachers have communes all over the world and people from different parts of the world visit them and stay there to learn the various techniques to expand their consciousness. However, with the passage of time and after the departure of enlightened Gurus, these communes are being commercialized and trying to run their operation as money making machines instead of helping people who are interested in raising their consciousness. Some of the communes have taken the shape of Meditation Universities or Spiritual Learning Centers.

Cosmic consciousness is above the human consciousness. After becoming cosmic conscious, a person attains a higher level of intellect, moral, spiritual, and charismatic image. The prime characteristic of cosmic consciousness is a consciousness of the cosmos- the life and order of universe. It is an enhancement of self- consciousness. Cosmic consciousness imparts intelligent, enlightenment or illumination which place an individual on a new plane of existence. It adds further moral exaltation, an ineffable feeling of elevation, elation, and joyousness. This leads to sense of immortality, a consciousness of eternal life. Great prophets fall in this category such as Jesus, Moses, Buddha, Rama, Krishna, Mahavira, Mohammed, and Guru Nanak Dev. Some scientists also possess to some degree of cosmic consciousness such as Albert Einstein, Max-Mueller, Edison, and Newton.

Philosophers like Socrates, Plato, Aristotle, and Dante also share some planes between self-consciousness and cosmic consciousness. There are different planes of existence with variable energies between the self-consciousness to cosmic consciousness. It must be clearly understood that all cases of cosmic consciousness are not on the same plane. One may be a prophet, the other may be mystic or a famous actor. Simple consciousness, self- consciousness and cosmic consciousness as each occupying a plane, then as the range of self-consciousness on its plane is far greater than the range of simple consciousness in any given species on its plane. Similarly, the range of cosmic consciousness is greater than that of self-consciousness. Men having cosmic consciousness vary in intellectual ability, moral character and spiritual elevation as compared to those inhabitants of a planet of self- consciousness. Energy spectrum from simple consciousness to self-consciousness to cosmic consciousness is composed of different energy levels. Souls' behavior in diverse levels of energy vary according to their plane of frequency.

As per Shri Shri Anand Murti, Indian yogi, philosopher and author, "Cosmic consciousness abides in one's sense of existence; in one's very heart's desire." Cosmic consciousness is the part of human beings that is capable of transcending to a higher level. It is the point of contact with God and the essence of being human. Higher consciousness establishes a distinction between the natural and the spiritual sides of human being. Some mystics understood cosmic consciousness to be collective consciousness, a larger reservoir of consciousness which manifests itself in the minds of people and remains intact after the dissolution of the individual. The experience of cosmic consciousness is incomplete without the element of love. It is the evolution of the intellect to higher self- consciousness. We become one with the Absolute and we become aware of our oneness. That all is one, means we are all connected to one source of Grand Unified Field of Energy.

Cosmic consciousness appears in an individual mostly of high intellect, high morals, courageous, positive thinking, with excellent physique and personality. It generally appears in early young life between the age of thirty and forty years when the individual is in his prime. However, there is no hard and fast rule, it can occur in later years too. There is a saying, "It is always summer in the soul". There is no specific time, nor age for the attainment of cosmic consciousness. First, there is a realization of the self-consciousness which transcends to cosmic consciousness. Both are at distinct levels.

Attainment of cosmic sense is seen by a sense of excitement. Its apprehension gives a feeling of insanity or delusion or hallucination. A person who enters cosmic consciousness belongs to the top phase of the self-consciousness and has extraordinary intellect. He must have a good physique, high moral character, strong sympathies, a warm heart, unconditional love, courage, strong moral commitments, and earnest spiritual feelings. With continued practice of spiritual discipline, one day he enters cosmic consciousness. The following are the characteristics of cosmic sense described by Vedanta philosophy and are illustrated in the Figure 6.

The person is suddenly immersed in colored clouds. Assorted color flashes across the eyes. He is full of joy, ecstasy, high morals and super intelligence. He feels the sense of immortality and eternal life. There is no fear of death. He feels connected with other living beings. There is an unconditional love for everybody instead of hate and jealousy. There is a sudden and instantaneous awakening which brings a clear view of many latent events. He comes out of duality. His entire life is changed and illuminated. His personality is absolutely changed. He develops a charismatic image. People are attracted to him. The transfiguration of the subject makes him divine. As per Dante, such a person is Trans humanized into a God. Bhagavad Gita, the holy books of the Hindus, illustrates, "The devotee, whose happiness is within himself, and whose light of knowledge also is within himself, becoming one with the Brahman, obtains the Brahmic bliss."

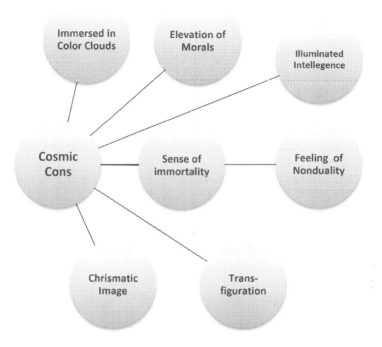

Figure 6: Characteristics of Cosmic Consciousness

4. Collective:

Collective consciousness or unity consciousness is the same. Collective consciousness means, we are all connected and have one source of consciousness. There is only one reality, one infinite source of endless consciousness comprising all living and non-living matter.

Consciousness is composed of many universes. Some of these universes are complex and some are relatively simple. Our earth planet is a very small portion of the universe. There are hundreds of billions of galaxies. Each one containing hundreds of billions of stars. One of the stars, is the Sun. The third planet from the Sun, is Planet Earth consisting of almost 7 billion humans. Each of us thinks he is separate from the other. But the entire universe is one.

Each soul is like a drop of water from the large ocean of consciousness. Very well voiced by Jaeda De Walt, an artist, photographer and author, "Each of us is a unique thread, woven into the beautiful fabric, of our collective consciousness."

All living and non-living objects are made of atoms, consisting of sub-atomic particles. These particles move in wave motion. In fact, all particles in the whole universe – are all composed of patterns in the same one infinite, universal energy field. One Grand Unified Field of Energy makes up everything in the whole universe. Our souls are parts of the Oneness that have agreed to co-create this illusion of separation which is called Duality. It is not real. Oneness is the only reality.

There is a saying, "as above, so below and as below, so above." This aphorism means, "Microcosm reflects the Macrocosm." Spirit in the creation of the cosmos, upon which all subsequent creation is patterned. In the centre of your being is the entire world. A simpler way of expressing this same idea is that "God is within you." The concept of non-duality, everything is One. That is the difference between collective and beings of duality consciousness. Unity consciousness means continuing to live in the world of duality with the understanding that is an illusion. We are all one with the source though we live, act, behave, think, and feel differently. Beings of duality consciousness are those who live in illusion. They choose to live, act, behave, think, feel and believe that they are separate from each other. It is very well expressed by Elkhart Toll, the most popular spiritual author and teacher, who put it in a wonderful way, "Each individual is an expression of the collective consciousness of humanity, and the collective consciousness of humanity is an expression of the one universal consciousness."

5. Absolute:

Absolute consciousness is eternal, invisible, self-illuminous, self-created yet omnipresent, without beginning or end. Absolute consciousness, is pure 'I'-an infinite Subject. All manifestations involve from it. Absolute consciousness is original, self-existent, and constitutive of all things. Absolute consciousness is without a subject and without an object. It means non-relative and non-conditioned. It is inert or unrelated to a cognizing entity and not concerned with any phenomenon. Param Brahman, the One Reality, the Absolute, is Absolute Consciousness.

Ultimately, all the forms of consciousness such as simple, human, collective and cosmic merge into one 'Absolute consciousness comprising the past, the present, and the future. Its essential nature is *total bliss*: it encompasses everything, living and nonliving.

Chapter Eight:

Consciousness and Mind

"All problems are illusions of the mind."
— Eckhart Tolle

It is described in the previous chapters that True-Self, Soul or *Atman* is absolute consciousness. However, human consciousness is influenced by mind and body. So, the experience of a human being is relative to the knowledge acquired. It remains changing due to thoughts. It remains in duality. Mind is restless due to constant thoughts and imagination. 'Self' has a dynamic power that it can assume the form of a formed consciousness. Thus, modification of the human consciousness is mind. Mind is the medium through which consciousness manifests-it is like a painting. The painting can never know the painter; likewise, mind can never know or define consciousness. Mind has limitation. Consciousness is without limitation and so remains untouched by mind. As per Abhijit Naskar, one of the world's celebrated Neuroscientists, "The human self and the God self are both creations of molecules in the human brain."

Mind has various faculties and centers and operates through corresponding physical centers in the brain. The brain is not mind as most of the people think. Mind is the seat of the physical brain. It gains experiences of this physical universe through the vibrations of the brain. Present discussion is only focused on the relation of mind with consciousness.

The human mind is restless. It is like a monkey who has been bitten by wasp. It is restless. It tends to go out and reach out to things and objects it likes. It is constantly changing. It is appalled with monotony. It withdraws and moves away from things it dislikes. Mind with its faculty comprising intellect, emotions, and ego has the tendency to evaluate, and judge, events and situations it encounters. It reacts to situations either positively or negatively.

Mind and Consciousness:

Mind is unpredictable, erratic and impulsive. It forgets every moment. It is changing every second. If food is withdrawn for a couple of days, it cannot think properly. There is no functioning of the mind during deep sleep. It is full of desires, lust and cravings. It is a storehouse of good and evil thoughts. It gets puzzled during anger. In fear, it trembles. In shock, it sinks. How can you take the mind, then, as the pure Self? It is not. Mind reacts quickly, consciousness does not. Mind attaches to materialistic objects, consciousness does not. Mind is not an object. Its existence is unseen. Its magnitude can't be measured. It requires no space. No localization. Mind precedes matter. Mind and matter are subject and object. Mind is all thoughts. Mind is nothing but a collection of the events of the past comprising unfulfilled desires, conflicts and experiences arising from contact with various objects. It is also a collection of feelings aroused by worldly problems. These desires, ideas, conflicts, and feelings are constantly changing. Some of the old desires and feelings are constantly departing from the mind, and new ones are replacing them. Thus, mind is mysterious.

Since mind is ever-changing, wavering, and unstable, it leads to many complications. Due to the thoughts of the past and worries for the future, mind is the cause for bondage, sufferings, and even liberation. A very common saying, *nothing is good or bad only thinking makes so.* Every man has a mental world of his own. Every man entirely differs from another man in mode of thinking, temperament, taste, feelings, and related emotions and they react differently to the same circumstances. In the educated, mind is active and well-defined; in the undeveloped, it is cloudy and dull. There are several zones in the mind just as there are various compartments in the brain for particular types of thought.

During intense anger, the whole mind is immersed with malice and ill-will. It hurts the person who shows anger too. During anger intellect does not work. Consciousness directly cognizes all the phenomena of the mind, viz., desire, imagination, doubt, belief, disbelief, shame, intelligence, and fear. Consciousness remains quite unattached and unaffected like the omnipresent ether, like the crystal which reflects different colored objects. All good and evil thoughts and implications of mind are depicted on the screen of consciousness.

Strong and the Weak Mind:

A strong mind has influence over the weak mind. A hypnotist with a strong mind can hypnotize people of weak minds. He who has purified his mind becomes a center of force. All the lesser, impure, weak minds are unconsciously drawn towards the purified, greater mind, because they derive peace, power and strength from the greater, purified mind. "If one conquers the mind, he conquers the world," is expressed by great Indian mystic Guru Nanak Dev.

A highly-developed mind always influences over a less developed mind. It is an amazing experience to be in the presence of a mystic master though he hardly speaks a word but creates a spell over other. Some strong minds are good orators too who can spellbind the audience with their art of thinking and speaking.

Mind and Food:

Upanishad emphasized, "When the food is pure, the whole nature of a man becomes pure; when the nature becomes pure, the memory becomes firm; and when a man is in possession of a firm memory, all the ties are severed." (*Chhandogya Upanishad vii-xxvi-2*)

Food has a direct and intimate connection with the mind and plays a vital role in the make-up of the mind. Simple diet calms the mind. Spicy diets excite the mind. According to Upanishad, the mind is derived from the subtle essence of food consumed which produces love, hatred, lust, pride, anger, jealousy and greed. In Sanskrit language, it is expressed as *Jasya bhojnam, tasyam manam* meaning *nature of mind depends upon the type of food one consumes.* That's why simple vegetarian food is recommended over non-vegetarian, spicy one. If the food is pure, thought also becomes pure. He who has pure thoughts speaks very powerfully and produces a deep impression on the minds of the listeners by his speech. He can influence thousands of persons through his pure thoughts.

Source of Mind:

Source of mind is consciousness. Who are you without a thought? The mind without any thought is pure awareness or consciousness. However, thoughts modified it, and mind becomes modified consciousness. Pure Consciousness or the Absolute Consciousness is common in all. This pure consciousness is one unified source of energy. All the workings of the mind, all modifications that arise in the minds of all are presented to the one common consciousness which is the witness of the mental thoughts. Even though consciousness is one, mind is different in every individual owing to different thoughts. It is mind that limits a man who is identical with the Supreme Soul. This identity is realized when the veil of ignorance is removed. In dreams, there is effulgent light. Where does it come from? It clearly explains, the Supreme Soul is self-luminous. As per Swami Sivananda, a great Indian mystic and one of the yoga masters of 20th century, "The source of mind is absolute consciousness, The Power of powers who gives power to the mind, the Light of lights who sheds light on the mind, the Seer of seers who witnesses the motives of and movements in the mind, the Support of supports on which the mind rests in sleep is soul or absolute consciousness."

The Kena Upanishad, the Vedic Sanskrit text book relates the same way about mind and consciousness. Activities of our senses and mind depend upon one source of eternal consciousness as expressed below.

"Not that which the eye can see,
but that whereby the eye can see.
Not that which the ear can hear,
but that whereby the ear can hear.
Not that which speech can illuminate,
but that by which speech can illuminated.
Not that which the mind can think,
but that whereby the mind can think.
Know 'That' to be Brahman the Eternal."

(The Kena Upanishads)

Features of Mind:
There are four aspects of mind such as Intellect, emotional mind, memory, and Ego.

Intellect: It is the part of the mind in which knowledge conceptual, judgment, reasoning, determination, discrimination, and perceptual appears as finished product.

Emotion: It is the part of mind with uncertainties such as doubts, guilt, blaming, lies, disappointment, hesitation, fear etc.

Memory: Remembering the impression of the past stored memories in the subconscious mind.

Ego: False sense of the doer, comparison, feeling of superiority over other.

Modification of Mind: The mind itself is the cause for the bondage of rebirth, when the mind is destroyed, everything is destroyed. When the mind manifests, everything is manifested. The Mind's modifications are classified as follows.

Turbid Mode: This mode causes confusion, fear, delusion, dullness etc.

Distracted Mode: This phase results in attachment, grief, passion, anger, desire for objects.

Transparent Mode: The person is full of compassion, patience, kindness, no desire for materialistic objects. He is noble, generous, charitable and upright.

The real happiness is achieved by the cessation of all modifications of mind. It is only when mind turns back the thoughts to their source.

Modification of the mind occurred by the appearance of any object. It can be caused by thoughts too. The senses such as sight, touch, hearing, smelling and taste can produce good or bad thoughts. If these modifications can be avoided, the seer realizes his true self. The seer abides in himself. The seer exists by itself as itself.

Mind also leads to duality. All knowledge is duality. Mind classifies things into desires and leads to pleasure and pain. The root cause of all pains is desire.

Thought as Mind:

Everything in the material universe had its origin first in thought, then in form, and later in action. Everything had its birth, its origin, first in the mind of the one who formed it before it received its material form. Before any action, first the thought is conceived in the mind. Repeated actions lead to the formation of habits and repeated habits define the character of a person.

The world is merely an idea or thought. When the mind ceases to think, the world vanishes and there is ineffable bliss. When the mind begins to think, immediately the world reappears and there is suffering. As per Descartes, *"Cogito, ergo sum—I think, therefore I am."* He personified thoughts. The universe is rendered visible by invisible mind. What is this invisibility? It is nothing except a bundle of thoughts and the thought 'I' is the root of all thoughts. This 'I' is a false idea, a non-entity. When the root of all thoughts vanishes into nothing, there is no mind. The first thought that arose in mind was 'Aham', 'I am'. The last thought that will arise in the mind before it is absorbed in Almighty will be that I am *Brahman*, means "I am God." What are you without a thought? Have you ever inquired?

Thought as Living Force:

Thought is a most vital, subtle, and irresistible force, that exists in the universe. The thought-world is more real relatively than the physical world. Thoughts are living things. Every change in thought is accompanied by vibrational energy. Thought as force needs a special kind of subtle matter in its working. Mind assumes the form of anything it contemplates. Many modifications continually arise in the mind. Thoughts rapidly change, and accordingly mind also changes. Every moment, mind is continually creating thousands of these thought-forms and continually dispersing them again. It never holds on steadily to one thought-form for some time. One moment it is here, the other moment in UK or in India.

Thought excels light in speed, while light travels at the rate of 186,000 miles per second, thoughts virtually travel in no time. Every thought has a certain name and a certain form. Form is the grosser and name the finer state of a single manifesting power called thought.

When the mind is calm, entirely without thought, there is no name and form. Nevertheless, as soon as a thought begins to rise, it will immediately take name and form. It is beautifully expressed by David Chalmers, an eminent philosopher, and cognitive scientist, "How does the water of the brain turn into the wine of consciousness?"

Thought as Subtle Matter:

Thought is subtle matter and lives a permanent impression in the mind. Thoughts never die and go with the soul. They have form, shape, color, quality, and power. A spiritual thought has yellow color; a thought charged with anger and hatred is of a dark red color; a selfish thought has a brown color; and so on.

Creative Power of Thoughts:

Thought is a great dynamic force. It is infectious and creative. Negative thoughts influence easily and rapidly. The power of thought is very great and valuable. The strength of the body, the strength of the mind, the success in life and the pleasures one gives to others by one's company— all depend on the nature and quality of maturity of thoughts. Thoughts can create destiny, imparts good health and build good moral character. On the other hand, negative thoughts can create havoc, too, mentally, physically and financially. As per Buddha, "Your worst enemy can't harm you as much as your own unguarded thoughts."

Each thought is a link in an endless chain of causes and effects, each effect becoming a cause and each cause having been an effect; and each link in the endless chain is welded out of three components— desire, thought and activity. A desire stimulates a thought; a thought creates itself as an act. Repeated acts institute in the formation of habits. Habits become the second nature of a person and network of destiny. Similarly, the character of an individual is formed. So, thoughts play a significant role in making and marring the life of an individual. Constructive thoughts can definitely shape the life and fortune of an individual. Everything is in the mind since mind is nothing but a collection of thoughts. There is nothing good or unpleasant, only thinking makes it so. The mind is a very powerful and irresistible force. If used wisely, it can take us to name and fame or even to heights of ecstasy. If not used wisely, it can enslave us and plunge us into miseries. As long as the mind is restlessly wandering amidst objects, ever fluctuating, excited, agitated and uncontrolled, true happiness cannot be recognized and attained. In fact, mind separates us from the absolute consciousness. Don't follow your mind blindly, it is not loyal to you. When you follow your thoughts, you follow a ghost. It is very imperative to analyze them with intellect. Susan L. Taylor, an American writer and journalist put it as, "Thoughts have power, thoughts are energy. And you can make your world or break it by your own thinking."

When we think of nothing our mind and heart are relaxed. But when we get hooked into a world of despair we're being drowned in a dark ocean of consciousness. To control the restless mind and perfectly still all thoughts is the hard-hitting problem of mankind which can be solved only by regular meditation and following strict physical, mental, moral, and spiritual disciplines.

Conclusion:

The relation between mind and consciousness is — mind is modified consciousness. The modification depends upon the type of thoughts the mind possesses. Without thoughts, there is no modified consciousness, only pure consciousness leading to *total bliss*. The seer realizes its true nature, abides in himself and exists by itself as itself. As per Sigmund Freud, Austrian neurologist and the founder of psychoanalysis, "Consciousness mind may be compared to a playing fountain in the sun and falling back into the subterranean pool of subconscious from which it rises."

Chapter Nine:

Ego, Ego-consciousness, and Consciousness

"The Ego is a veil between humans and God'."
— *Jalaluddin Rumi*

The ego is known in Sanskrit language as *Ahamkar,* which means vanity or self-esteem –a form of 'I am'- self of any person. In fact, it is the Latin word for 'I' which is the sense of ego. Sense of 'I' binds all sensations, perceptions, concepts, and feelings. Each individual ego is an individual center which calls itself 'I'. If a person is using too much 'I' expression in his talks such as, I did this, I did that, and I am so and so. It is an indication of Ego. In other words, if a person has an excessively favorable opinion of one's own ability, intellect, or importance, he is egoistic. When you say, someone has a big ego then you are saying the person is too full of himself. His or her supremacy or self-esteem creates problems for his or her progress in his profession and in day to day life as well. His interaction with his colleagues and nears and dears would be unpleasant. Ego is the only requirement to destroy relations. Man, only remains hypnotized with the false idea of an ego. When this illusion vanishes, then Self only exists. A man once asked the Buddha, "I want happiness." The Buddha replied, "First remove 'I', that's ego. Then remove 'want'— That's desire. And now all you're left with is happiness.

Ego cannot be perceived by the senses unless it assumes certain forms or characteristics. To comprehend ego, it is very pertinent to know its origin, forms, nature, and dissolution (Figures 7 & 8).

Origin and Formation of the Ego:

The origin of ego is with the start of thoughts and formation of 'I' in an individual. The moment a child starts saying 'I', ego is formed. Ego is very natural and essential phenomenon in human being.

Figure 7: Various forms of Ego

Nature of the Ego:

This sense of 'I' makes an individual entity or personality. It imparts certain amount of steadiness and equipoise to the conscious process. It leads to an understanding of duality. The phase is temporary and vanished by the growth of human consciousness. Ego-centered integration is based on illusion since the ego-consciousness thinks itself as the body. I am this, I am that. Ego causes conflicts. All materialistic comforts such as power, fame, and wealth, are essential for it. It gets attached to them. On the other hand, true spirituality is essential to pure consciousness (true self) but ego-consciousness looks upon it as insignificant. Ego causes separateness through craving, desire, hate, anger, fear, discrimination, intolerance, and jealousy.

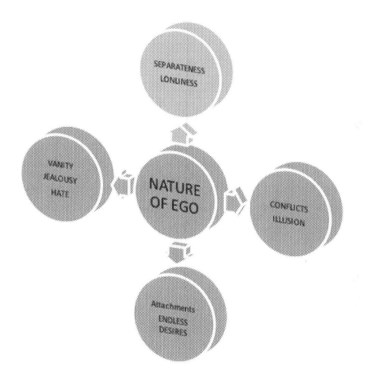

Figure 8: Nature of Ego

The person is left out due to these properties. All these characteristics lead to duality. The only remedy to minimize separateness is to love His manifestation.

All kinds of Ego forms can be dissolved by unconditional love only. The problem of dissolving the ego from consciousness is very complicated because the roots of ego are hidden in the subconscious mind. The ego is like an iceberg floating in the sea. About one-seventh of the ice-berg remains above the surface of the water, and major portion is submerged into the water. Similarly, only a small portion of the ego is apparent and the major portion of the ego remains submerged in the dark, in the subconscious mind. Complete eradication of the ego is possible only when all the constituents of the ego pass through the fire of intelligent consciousness. Vanity is another feeling through which egoism reveals. Ego is activated by the principle of self-perpetuation too. Moreover, it comes with life naturally. The ego has no judgement of its own, it is objective and depends upon what it has seen and heard from others. Sound judgement can only be made without the interference of ego. The state of egoism must be free from the mind for self-realization. Ego is like algae deposited by running water in a drain. To get a proper flow from the drain, it needs to be cleared regularly. It is owing to this ego, which is like algae, the true nature of our inner self is veiled and cannot be revealed.

Relation among Senses, Mind, Intellect, Ego and Consciousness:

To know the concept of ego, we must understand the relationship among the senses, mind, intellect, and consciousness (True self). Assume your body like a chariot as illustrated in Figure 9. The rider is your consciousness, the five horses are your five senses. The driver is your intellect, and the mind is the reins. Desires of the senses are the roads, where these horses are running. If the rider is your consciousness (true self) which is eternal and immortal part of your own self, it is not affected by any sensation of duality such as pleasure or pain but the ego-consciousness is affected. The thinker, the doer, and the knower of pain is not the consciousness but it is the thinking, eating, drinking and working man. It is the ego which is permeated with I-consciousness. Then there comes another sense which is still higher than the determining faculty (intelligence). That is the sense of I, *me* and *mine*. It is the ego which is impregnated with I-consciousness. Behind the ego there is a rider the true consciousness. *This ego, a combination of the intellect, the mind, senses and consciousness (true self) is known as Ego-consciousness (Ego-Cons).*

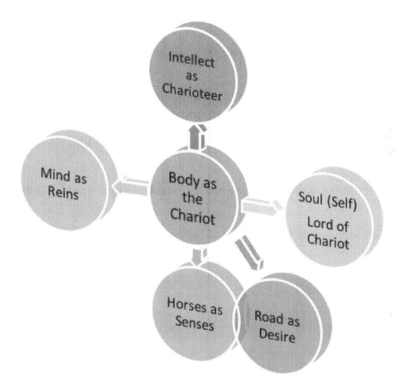

Figure 9: Relationship of senses, mind, intellect, and true self

A majority of the people think, 'I' as the body and get attached to materialistic things. My family, my children, my house, my property, this is all mortal ego. In other words, immortal entity forms the mortal entity ego-cons who thinks and feels. Now the charioteer is the determining power for all the good or bad things done or received. If he is not careful the horses (senses) drag the chariot down into the ditch. The horses will be out of control if the driver is not strong. If the driver (intellect) does not know how to manage the horses (senses), the ego-cons will suffer. If the driver (intellect) knows the right path, or manage the horses even on a tough path, there will be no sufferings, and sorrow. If the reins (mind) are weak, the driver can't help. So, a strong mind is also very essential. A vast majority of people have no control over their horses (senses) and will get into all kinds of troubles such as robbery, theft, cheating, murder, adultery, rapes, and related criminal activities. If one can hold the reins of the mind firmly and use the power of discrimination (intellect) and understanding properly, he will have no problem, no matter where he goes.

In order to achieve the right power of determination, we must purify ourselves, purify our minds, senses, and exercise self–control. Impure thoughts and impure ideas lead us to misery. Understand the physical, moral, mental, and spiritual disciplines properly and live up to those standards. This will lead to perfection, a state in which all the senses and passion are under control. In the state of perfection, past, present, and future will be equally revealed to an individual. A person can understand his true nature and its relationship to the infinite *Being*. All vital questions like the nature of infinite, *Being*, its source and history, and the roots of all phenomena will be solved at that stage. Three conditions are required for achieving the highest end in life. These are self-control, self-denial, and right knowledge. After achieving these qualities, the person attains self-realization that will lead to God realization.

Ego-consciousness:

In view of the above, it is revealed that Ego-consciousness is a combination of senses, mind, intellect, and (consciousness) true-self as shown in Figure 10. As long as the ego-consciousness is dominating in an individual, the connection to his consciousness is impassable. Ego-cons takes over the true consciousness, and pretends itself to be the True Self or consciousness. In reality, it is an ego-consciousness or ego self.

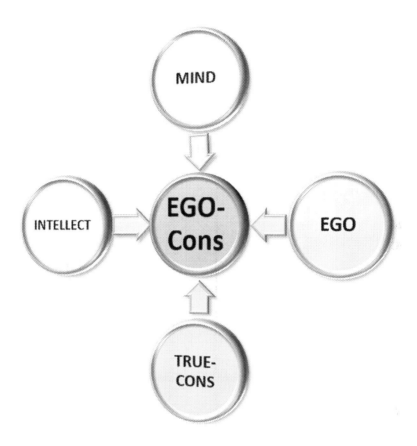

Figure 10: Formation of Ego-Consciousness

The merging of the ego and consciousness is known from the beginning of human consciousness and played a significant role in the evolution of human consciousness. That means to recognize and organize the experiences based on ego to transform into ego-consciousness. Ego-consciousness is present in the waking state, dreaming, and sleeping states of an individual. It pretends to be the real self where as in reality it is not. Since ego-consciousness is composed of mind, intellect, and body, it can be recognized based on its distinct form and qualities. It is modified with the mind. It envelops the soul with thoughts, events, and memories and prevents it from shining. The ego-consciousness suffers as it influenced by the objective world. It enters a state of objectivity by identifying itself with various objects. It remains there and gets attached to the materialistic world and does not want to come out even in extreme circumstances. It extends itself into the illusionary world (Maya) through the mind and the senses. Ego-consciousness is contaminated with desires, instincts, emotions, thoughts, impressions, and memories. It is like a mirror covered with dust.

Some drastic experiences of the ego-consciousness leave latent impressions and accompany the soul to the next birth. As per Vedanta, the ego-cons is subject to the five limitations of space, time, knowledge, power, and happiness. As long as the ego-cons lives in its natural form, there is no escape for the soul from its physical existence. The bodily consciousness is held as prisoner and is influenced by the mind with all kinds of mental formations and objective knowledge.

The innermost part of all the spiritual teachings recommends to eliminate ego by surrendering vanity and accepting humility. By letting go of the self-referential term 'I' as a habit of thinking, the ego will be lessened. Substitute the habit of expressing ideas in the third person instead of with the subjective pronoun 'I'. Choose to be easygoing, benign, forgiving, compassionate, unconditional love for everyone, unselfish service, and respectful to all. Seek to understand and appreciate rather to criticize. Avoid negativity, expectation from other, greed, lust, and the desire for materialistic life. Leave the habit of opinionating, judgment of right and wrong, and the trap of righteousness. These reforms will set you free from the necessary evil of ego.

All the reforms and practices are meant for the ego-cons. Inner self or true consciousness is complete, never changes, pure and immutable consciousness keeps the body alive. Therefore, nature makes sure that the soul is held tightly so that ego-cons can continue its existence and keep performing its normal duties. Our ego-cons is what we are right now. It should not be mistaken by the pure consciousness. They are two distinct entities. Ego-cons is active in the first three states of consciousness — waking state, dream state, and dreamless state — and fully asleep in the deep sleep state.

The ego-cons is dynamic. The true consciousness is passive witnessing soul. It lives only for a time in its entirety. It is eternal, unborn, and immortal. Ego-cons is outgoing and dispersive. Consciousness is self-absorbed and self-contained. Ego-con interacts with sense organs. Pure consciousness interacts with none. It is absolute. Ego-cons interact with the object and accumulate knowledge. The residual self is formed out of the ego-self, and goes with the soul to the next birth, and becomes the seed for the next Ego-self or Ego-cons. Ego-cons cannot be transformed completely to real-self even after purification and transformation.

When the ego-cons is purified through the practice of yoga and cultivation of truthful life, it becomes silent and stabilized. Then it reflects the brilliance of the pure consciousness.

Consciousness and Ego-cons in the Body:

As per Upanishad, we have two Selves— seers and seen or knower and known. They are just like two golden birds sitting on the same branch of the tree, intimate friends, the ego-self, and the true self dwell in the same body. The former eats the sweet and sour fruits of the tree of life while the latter looks on in detachment. One watches silently whereas the other is engaged in various actions. As long as we think we are the ego, we feel attached and fall into sorrow. But realize you are the self, the lord of life, and you will be freed from sorrow. When you realize that you are the absolute consciousness

(True self) supreme source of light, supreme source of love, you transcend the duality of life and enter unitive state of non-duality *(Mundaka Upanishad 3:1-3).* Yoga sutra describes the former as seer and the latter as the seen. Seer is the subject and seen is the object. Ignorance does not know the distinction between the two. Delusion is mistaking one for the other. Salvation is when the distinction between the two, the subject, and the object disappears and only the seers remain,

Consciousness and Ego-consciousness:

There is no sense of 'I' in true consciousness. True Self or consciousness is that part of you which is connected to a higher being, while ego is that sense of self-importance that you have when you compare yourself with others. True consciousness (soul) is something typically associated with positive emotions, while ego-self is attributed to negative emotions. Consciousness (soul) is secured and quiet, while ego is loud and self-important. The consciousness has no form but ego-cons has. The consciousness is eternal while the ego-self lasts for brief time. Consciousness is absolute, where ego-cons changes continuously. Consciousness is passive and self-absorbed. Ego-cons is dynamic and outgoing. The true consciousness is not subject to the cycle of birth and death. It is self-aware and self-absorbed even when it is held in the body. It is not limited to time and space. The consciousness (soul) is pure. Calm, detached and radiant. It is not subject to any sufferings. Ego-cons goes from one birth to another and limited to time and space. It experiences sufferings through the mind and body owing to its wants, desires and actions. If we silence our thoughts comprising desires, attachments, impulses, feelings, emotions, memories, names, and forms, we can realize ourselves. Mind will be totally blank and only 'I am' is left alone. Some think it as witnesses of consciousness and some experience it as bliss consciousness. Maharishi Raman said, "By constantly keeping one's attention on the Source, the ego is dissolved in that Source like a salt-doll in the sea."

Ego-cons and consciousness (self) are two different identities. As long as the ego-cons is there self-realization is not possible. Transformation of ego-cons is the key to self-realization. This is only possible when ego-cons is devoid of ego and leaves the 'consciousness' alone which can be attained by right awareness, right knowledge, detachment, morality, purity, devotion and surrender to consciousness (self). It is very nicely expressed by Albert Einstein, "More the ego, lesser the knowledge, more the knowledge, lesser the ego".

Self-Realization and Ego-cons:

Self-realization means to understand the ego-cons and real consciousness as two different identities. It can be achieved by right awareness, proper knowledge, and intellect. It is also very important to know that ego-cons can never become real consciousness even in a person who is a perfect master. Ego-cons comprises of the impressions of many births and it is very difficult to get rid of them. So, what we see in an ordinary person is the reflection of his accumulated egoistic thinking and behavior. Complete purification and transformation of ego-cons is very essential for self-realization. This process will end the cycle of births and deaths and allowing the self finally free which is not easy. The ego-cons is involved in worldly materialistic desires and affairs like a tree whose roots are deep and entangles all over the place.

According to Hindu scriptures the soul is surrounded by four distinct sheaths; the physical body, the breath body, the mental body, and the intelligence body. The soul is bliss body, the innermost one. The sheath of four bodies comprise the ego-cons cover the soul and part of it leaves the body as residual ego and accompanies the consciousness (soul) after death. It remains attached to the soul for the duration of its stay in the next world and becomes the seed for the formation of the next ego-cons. The purification of the ego-cons through mind and body is the only way to get rid of this cycle which can be achieved by strictly following the physical, intellectual, moral, and spiritual disciplines. Maharishi Raman expressed in a very simple way, "If there is anything besides the 'Self' there is reason to fear? Who sees the second? First, the ego arises and sees objects as external. If the ego does not rise, the 'Self' alone exists and there is no second."

Chapter Ten:

Does Consciousness Survive Death?

"The soul can never be cut to pieces by any weapon, nor burned by fire, nor moistened by water, nor withered by the wind."

— *Bhagavad Gita.*

The quest to know life beyond death has always been a most fascinating one from time immemorial. The question of life after death has remained an enigma through the ages. It is a very intriguing and mysterious question everybody wants to know its answer. However, it is beyond the comprehension of human knowledge to explain this riddle. Nevertheless, the human mind would not accept any mystic answer without any reasonable conclusion. The demand of the time is for concrete evidence, not of solitary prodigies. All religions and spiritual traditions have their own concepts. There have been many theories on this subject. Some of them are based on religious principles, whereas the other on philosophical ones.

Most of the religions believe there is a "heaven" and "hell." Souls travel to heaven or hell after death of the body and awarded heaven or hell according to their good and bad deeds respectively. There is a detailed description of heaven and hell, too. However, the question arises, who has seen heaven and hell? Is there any proof? The concept of heaven and hell was introduced by some religions in order to create fear in the minds of people to refrain from crimes. Some of the Vedanta books also described the journey of the soul after death. A very interesting journey is described comprising the soul travelling through the ether, air, smoke, mist, cloud, and moon. Again, is there any proof of this journey? The description about the journey of the soul appears to be like fantasies. Most of the scientists have rejected such claims for lack of scientific data. Science relies principally on documentable facts and replicable evidence. Survival of the human consciousness after the death of the body is a very complex and unknown phenomenon. Most of the information was collected based on near death experiences (NDE) and reincarnation evidences. Most of them were on individual experiences. It is not easy to collect replicable proof.

Scientists have explored the biology behind 'out-of-body' experiences. They wanted to find out exactly what happens in the brain and the consciousness after the clinical death of the body.

When the heart stops beating no blood gets to your brain, and after about 10 seconds brain activity ceases. That is normally the official death point. Yet around 10% or 20% of people who are brought back to life from that point, which may be a few minutes or over an hour, report having consciousness. They all report being able to see what is happening. The scientists want to confirm whether these are real experiences or hallucinations, by cross-checking what the patients report that they saw happening from above, with the doctors and nurses who were present. They even revealed the conversations among the doctors and nurses. So far, hundreds of cases have been confirmed as accurate, to the astonishment of the medical staff.

If the rest of the study continues in the same direction, it will confirm that *consciousness continues even when the brain is not functioning.* In other words, consciousness is something separate from the physical brain and body. Christof Koch, the Chief Scientific Officer of the Allen Institute of Brain Science, and Lois and Victor Troendle, Professor of Cognitive and Behavioral Biology at California Institute of Technology, argued that the soul dies and everything is lost when human beings lose consciousness. "You lose everything.

The world does not exist anymore for you. Your friends don't exist anymore. You don't exist. Everything is lost."

Bruce Greyson, Professor of Psychiatry at the University of Virginia, challenged Koch's view of consciousness. He said that, "If you take these near-death experiences at face value, then they suggest that the mind or the consciousness seems to function without the physical body."

Latest research shows that consciousness survives after physical organs stop functioning. Studies prove the mind does not die with the body. "Scientists at the University of Southampton have spent four years examining more than 2,000 people who suffered cardiac arrests at 15 hospitals in the UK, US and Austria. They found that nearly 40 per cent of people who survived, described some kind of 'awareness' during the time when they were clinically dead before their hearts were restarted."

Sam Parnia, Director of Resuscitation Research at Stony Brook University, School of Medicine and one of the world's leading experts on the scientific study of death, says, "We're pushing through the boundaries of science here, working against assumptions and perceptions that have been fixed. A lot of people hold this idea that when you die, you die; that's it. Death is a moment — you know you're either dead or alive. All these things are not scientifically valid, but they are social perceptions. A new science is needed to explore this mystery."

A multi-disciplinary team was led by Sam Parnia to investigate an objective look at what happens to mind/consciousness during and after death. Their findings revealed as follows: "The evidence thus far suggests that in the first few minutes after death, consciousness is not annihilated. Whether it fades away afterwards, we do not know, but right after death, consciousness is not lost. We know the brain can't function when the heart has stopped beating. But in this case *conscious awareness appears to have continued for up to three minutes into the period when the heart wasn't beating*, even though the brain typically shuts down within 20-30 seconds after the heart has stopped. This is significant, since it has often been assumed that experiences in relation to death are likely hallucinations or illusions, occurring either before the heart stops or after the heart has been successfully restarted, but not an experience corresponding with 'real' events when the heart isn't beating. Furthermore, the detailed recollections of visual awareness in this case were consistent with verified events." Sam and his team want to pursue their study from a scientific and medical perspective rather than approaching it from a religious or philosophical point of view. He has described in his book, *Erasing Death, The Science that is rewriting the Boundaries between Life and Death,* that there is a continuation of consciousness after physical death and modern science can reverse the phenomenon of death.

Most of the findings are based on near death experiences which have not only little scientific plea but are also subjective and impossible to quantify. The scientists admit that they still don't know what is going on with human consciousness after death, even though the studies give concrete evidence that the consciousness is able to survive at least the first few minutes of bodily death, and maintain sufficient awareness to observe the clinically dead body and its surroundings while awaiting resuscitation.

Very recently, scientists claim that quantum theory proves, consciousness moves to another universe at death. A book entitled, *Biocentrism: How Life Consciousness are the keys to Understanding the Nature of the Universe* has perplexed the scientists. It reveals that life does not end when the body dies, and it can last forever. The author of the book *Robert Lanza* is an eminent scientist who believes in this theory of biocentrism that means life and consciousness are fundamental to the universe. Consciousness creates the material universe, not the material creates the consciousness. The research is a scientific clue that consciousness survives clinical death, and while not all that conclusive, the study certainly opens the door for an expanding understanding of the relationship between the body and the soul. Man possesses within himself infinite possibilities. The unlimited source of power and wisdom is within him. He must unfold the divinity within.

The Soul will continue to exist after death. Before this birth, an individual has passed through countless lives. The Lord Krishna says in the Bhagavad Gita, "O Arjuna, both you and I have had many births before this; only I know them all, while you do not. Birth is inevitably followed by death, and death by rebirth. As a man casting off worn-out garments taketh new ones, so the dweller in the body, casting off worn-out bodies, entered into others that are new."

The Upanishad text of Hindu philosophy also proclaims, "Just as a caterpillar which has come to the top of a blade of grass, draws itself over to a new blade, so also does the soul draw itself over to a new body, after it has put aside its old body"—Just as a goldsmith, having taken a piece of gold, makes another form, new and more beautiful, so also, verily the Atman or soul having cast off this body and having put away ignorance, makes another new and more beautiful form (Brihadaranyaka Upanishad).

Stephen Hawley Martin, a professional editor and celebrated author, also strongly believed that consciousness survived death and life force came to physical dimension for a reason. He described in his book entitled, *The Science of Life after Death*, many examples of eminent scientists who believed that life exists after death. Ample information available in the book on Near Death Experience also indicates human consciousness lives on. The science of reincarnation along with the cosmology of soul evolution are also illustrated in the book.

Raymond Moody, award winning author of a very popular book, *Life after Life,* also tried to emphasize that consciousness is metaphysical and survives death. Raymond Moody continues to draw enormous public interest and generates controversy with ground breaking work on the near-death experience and what happens when we die.

Robert Monroe, vice president of NBC Radio after leaving NBC, became famous for his research into altered states of consciousness. His book, *Journey Out of the Body* is very popular and also emphasized that human consciousness lives on. The book coined the term out of body experience (OBE). In fact, the term 'out of body experience' was first introduced in 1943 by George Tyrrell, a famous English parapsychologist, in his book, *Apparitions.* Later, the term was adopted by other researchers.

Professor Carl Jung, an eminent scientist and philosopher, suffered clinical death in 1944. He had cardiac arrest and no blood was passing to the brain. Doctors revived him by injecting adrenaline into his heart muscle, which started beating again. He described his out of body experience (OBE) in his book, *Memories, Dreams and Reflections.* Jung recalls his delightful experience, "It seems to me that I was high up in the space. Far below, I saw the globe of the earth bathed in a glorious blue light. I saw the deep blue sea and the continents. Far below my feet lay Ceylon, and the distance ahead of me the subcontinent of India. My field of vision did not include the whole earth, but its global shape was plainly distinguishable and its outlines shone with a silvery gleam through that wonderful blue light. In many places, the globe seemed colored or spotted dark green like oxidized silver. Far away to the left lay a broad expanse the reddish yellow desert of Arabia. It was though the silver of the earth had there assumed a reddish-gold hue. Then came the Red Sea, and far, far back—as if in the upper left of the map—I could just make out a bit of the Mediterranean. My gaze was directed chiefly towards that. Everything else appeared indistinct. I could also see the snow-covered Himalayas, but in that direction, it was foggy or cloudy. I did not look to the right at all. I knew that I was on the point of departing from the earth. Later, I discovered how high in space one would have to be to have so extensive a view – approximately a thousand miles. The sight from the earth from this height was the most glorious thing I had ever seen."

Stephen Braude, an American philosopher, parapsychologist and Editor in Chief of the *Journal of Scientific Exploration*, and a Professor of philosophy at the University of Maryland, believed that life existed beyond death. His book, *Immortal Remains*: *The Evidence for Life after Death*, is quite interesting and reveals some facts for demonstrating how life continues after death.

Eben Alexander, a famous neurosurgeon who performed over 100 brain surgeries, described his own experience in his book, *Proof of Heaven* that consciousness survived death. He contracted bacterial meningitis in the year 2008. The deadly infection paralyzed his brain and sent him into a coma. His entire neocortex, the outer surface of the brain, the part that makes us human was entirely shut down. His attending doctors gave only a 5 percent chance for his survival. He came out of the coma after a week and revived his consciousness within 36 hours and able to read his illness charts. He was reborn. He narrated his near-death experience, "During my seven days of coma, I not only remained fully conscious, journeyed to a stunning world of beauty and peace and unconditional love…I underwent the most staggering experience of my life, my consciousness travelling to another level." He further explained, "Our spirit is not dependent on the brain or body. It is eternal and no one has one sentence worth of hard evidence that it isn't."

However, his colleagues were not convinced with his experience. For years, Eben Alexander had never accepted near death experiences. He was, after all, a neurosurgeon with sophisticated training and good reputation. But his severe brain infection and recovery transformed his life completely.

Science can reveal information about matter, but it is absolutely helpless as far as the world of consciousness is concerned. Science has been denying the presence of consciousness in the past but now struggling to investigate it by developing sophisticated techniques to study the brain, though neuroscience. However, it failed to understand as to how the material brain produces the immaterial sense of consciousness or true awareness.

Osho an Indian thinker, controversial mystic, and spiritual teacher, stated, "All that can be experienced is not necessarily explainable, and all that can be explained is not necessarily experienceable. Mathematics can be explained easily, but there is no corresponding experience. Science can be explained easily, but even the greatest scientist is not transformed by his knowledge."

During the end of the 19th century, physicists had been working with Newton's laws of motion. They were satisfied while applying these laws to their further researches. However, these laws do not make sense while studying the motion at the subatomic level. This gave birth to a new physics called Quantum Physics. There have been many studies to investigate consciousness through quantum physics. It is successful to some extent but still science could not find the reason of survival of consciousness after the brain is shut off.

The real fundamental concept is that we ignore consciousness, and identify ourselves to our body. Body is only a resting place, like an inn. It will perish one day but our pilgrimage is eternal. Being in the body one can become identified, one can start thinking, "I am the body." "I am the mind." This is happening more and more in the modern materialistic world.

According to science, consciousness is illusion, body is the only reality. The truth is that the body has its own reality, and consciousness has its own reality. The miracle is, that these two separate realities are together, and are functioning in deep synchronicity.

As one goes deeper into this philosophy, he will be able to realize that if the hand is cut off, consciousness is not reduced. It remains the same. If the leg is cut off; body is no longer the same, but his consciousness remains the same. If one's mind changes, his consciousness does not change. It is the only unchanging; everything else is in a flux. Only the witness remains permanent and eternal. Mind is time, whereas consciousness is timelessness.

Death does not destroy anything. The five elements of the body fall back into their original sources and for the consciousness there are two possibilities: if it has some desires left, it will move into another womb; if it has known its eternity, its immortality, it will move into the cosmos and disappear into this vast existence. He has become one with the source. This is called *Nirvana or Moksha.*

Conclusion:

A conscientious person knows there is no death. The Soul is immortal. Death does not happen; it has never happened. It happens only when one is identified with the body and he doesn't know himself. Yes, from the body he will be separated and separation looks like death. But if one is not identified with the body and he knows himself as the witnessing soul, as the pure consciousness, as the pure awareness, then there is no death. It is an interval between the existing life and the next life. In summation, why people do worry about life after death, why don't they enjoy life they have now and forget the past and the future. On the other hand, if consciousness can survive and act independently of the body during one's life time, it can surely survive after death. It is very appropriate to quote here Stanislav Grof, a Czech psychiatrist, "Whether or not we believe in survival of consciousness after death, reincarnation, and karma, it has very serious implications for our behavior."

Chapter Eleven:

Reincarnation of Human Consciousness

"As a man, casting off worn out garments taketh new ones, so the dweller in the body, entered into ones that are new."
— *Bhagavad Gita*

Reincarnation is a very concrete proof that consciousness survives death. The doctrine of reincarnation of souls is a fundamental dogma of Hinduism and Buddhism. The ancient Egyptian and the Greek also believed in reincarnation. Emerson, Plato, Pythagoras had absolute conviction in this philosophy.

As per Dalai Lama, spiritual leader of the Tibetan people, "Reincarnation is not an exclusively Hindu and Buddhist concept, but it is part of the history of human origin. It is proof of the mind-stream's capacity to retain knowledge of physical and mental activities. It is related to the theory of independent origination and to the law of cause and effect."

Reincarnation was accepted for the first 500 years' history of the church and later was condemned by the Council of Constantinople. Reincarnation is considered by many Christians to be against Christians Doctrine in the United States. About 25 per cent of Christians believe in reincarnation. In 1959, Great Britain showed 12% of the people believed in reincarnation. The Figures had grown to 28% in 1979. Today, the concept of reincarnation is widely accepted throughout the world.

When we talk about reincarnation, some of the questions perplexed us such as who are we? Where do we come from? Where do we go from here? Why are we here? Scientists and philosophers are still struggling to find the answers of these questions. Osho, an Indian mystic stated, "The real question is not whether life exists after death. The real question is whether you are alive before death."

Stuart Hameroff, who proposed the highly controversial Orch-OR (orchestrated objective reduction) theory of consciousness in 1996 along with Roger Penrose, told the *Science* channel, "I think the quantum approach to consciousness can, in principle, explain why we're here and what our purpose is, and also the possibility of life after death, reincarnation and persistence of consciousness after our bodies give up." He has been assiduously working on this subject but nothing conclusive has been revealed so far.

Eben Alexander, a neurosurgeon, wrote the widely circulated and criticized book, *Proof of Heaven*. He described his own experience in this book. He said, "I have a great belief and knowledge that there is a wonderful existence for our souls outside of this earthly realm and that is our true reality, and we all find that out when we leave this earth." Eben Alexander says that he traveled through this heaven, surrounded by "millions of butterflies," with a woman. This woman gave him three messages: "You are loved and cherished, dearly, forever," "You have nothing to fear" and "There is nothing you can do wrong."

Reincarnation studies have been done by Ian Stevenson, Director of the Division of Personality Studies at the University of Virginia. Stevenson has devoted the last forty years to the scientific documentation of past life memories of children from all over the world. He studied over 3,000 cases. Many people, including skeptics and scholars, agree that these cases offer the best evidence for reincarnation.

Near death experiences (NDE) have been described by the patients in the hospitals during their surgical operations including brain, heart attacks and related critical conditions. Patients have narrated every detail of the actions in the operation theater including the conversations among the nurses and doctors operating upon them. Most of them even saw their body being worked on while standing outside the body.

Birth defects, birth marks, and fatal wounds like gun shots related to the past life have been observed in many people.

Extraordinary qualities or talents in education, music, sports, acting such as playing some musical instruments, singing, or knowing some languages, best sportsman at a very young age indicate past life expertise. A Russian lady called Tati Valo claims to have proof of reincarnation. She is said to be able to speak one hundred and twenty languages and believes that many of them are from previous lives. It is not easy to learn so many languages in one life. Suddenly, she remembered all the languages in a mathematics class and completely forgotten Russian language.

Fear of fire, fire arm, water, and heights in children and adults relate to the cause of death in their past life. Fear of Fire—if someone died in fire; fire arm— died by gunshot; fear of water—died by drowning; height—died by falling from the cliff or top of building etc., etc. Aversion or liking to some foods also refers to past life experiences. Perverted or sexual activities in children at an early age are attributed to their past life habits. Bad habits, stealing, lying, gambling, strange behavior during early childhood also are considered to the impressions of past life experiences.

Gillian Anderson, an American-British film actress, activist and writer said, "My whole life belief system is that our paths are drawn for us. I believe in reincarnation. I believe we're here to learn and grow. We choose how we come into this life based on what it is we have to learn. Some people have harder lessons than others."

The word reincarnation literally means embodiment again, coming again into a physical body. The individual soul takes again a fleshy covering. The word transmigration means passing from one place to another-passing into a new body. It is called *Samsara* in Vedanta.

The Sanskrit term *Samsara* is derived from the Sanskrit root *Sr,* which means—to pass-. The prefix *Sam* means—intensely. The individual soul passes repeatedly through this world and other subtle higher worlds. This repeated passing of souls—*Samsriti*—is what is really meant by the term *Samsara.* Samsara exists in order that the individual soul may learn to realize itself. Yogananda Paramhansa, an Indian yogi and Guru who introduced millions of westerners to the teachings of meditation and Kriya Yoga through his book, *Autobiography of a Yogi,* said, "Reincarnation is the law of spiritual evolution. It gives everything a chance to work out of its Karma (the law of action). Evolution and reincarnation are methods of propelling all creation towards final freedom in spirit, held no longer under the law of natural law of death."

What is the law that governs transmigration? Is it an automatic system? Who decides that? Some are born into rich families, where others are born into poor families. Some are born into rich countries where others are born into very poor countries. Some people have a very short life, some have long life. Some can survive in drastic circumstances where others die even in healthy environments. One is born blind. One is born handicapped, the other is born healthy. One is handsome, the other is ugly. One is genius and sharp. One is talented, the other is retarded and so on. There are lots of disparities. Why? Is there any law that governs life and death? Do human beings come here and pass out without any definite purpose? Is there no role of genetics in these factors?

The cause is the unmanifested condition of the effect whereas the effect is the manifested state of cause. A tree is the cause and a seed is the effect. The morphological and chemical constituents of a tree: how it looks and what types of phytochemicals are being biosynthesized by it, are stored in the tiny seed in potential energy. This tiny seed will give rise to the same physical and chemical properties after it attains the form of a big tree again. The active chemical constituents would almost remain the same. The seed of a mango tree will produce a mango tree only not a banana tree. Similarly seeds of the apples will produce an apple tree not a peach tree and so on. Likewise, the whole human form remains in the drop of a semen in an invisible potential form. It produces only a human being nothing else. In the case of a human, its consciousness is in a higher stage. It goes for reincarnation. Within the gross physical human body there is another subtle body called astral body. It is invisible and comprises all the impressions and tendencies of the mind.

After the death of the body, the astral body transmigrates to another body with all the impressions of the previous life. This remanifestation of the subtle form into gross physical form is called the law of reincarnation. Every child is born with certain characteristics related to past conscious actions. Goethe, the eminent German poet, was the master of seventeen languages. These cannot be acquired in one life. There must be some effect of previous lives. Similarly, Ludwig Van Beethoven, a German composer and Pianist was deaf but used to compose extraordinary symphony music.

Likewise, we can make the same statement about eminent scientists, Albert Einstein, Tasla and Edison and many other born genii. There are many stories such as citing a boy of five becomes an expert in piano. There had been boy-mathematician etc. This is not a miracle of nature but result of past life and can be explained.

If a person gets deep grooves in mind by learning music, musical instrument mathematics or any medical science in this birth, he or she carries these impressions in quantum state to the next birth and starts showing extraordinary talents during their childhood.

Heredity and ecological variations can explain certain things but cannot explain all these variations and diversities. Most of the time parents do not possess these qualities. Many intelligent parents have children with dull intellect or vice versa. It is a clear indication of past life experience. If the desires are not fulfilled in this life, the person has to come back again and again to earth-planet for their fulfilment. If one has an ardent desire to become an actor and he could not achieve it and he still cherishes this desire. This desire will bring him back to life and place him in suitable environments and favorable circumstances to become an actor. Now the question arises as to why we do not remember our past. The possible answer is, since we pass through many lives, it is not possible to remember any of them. We will go insane if all those memories stay with us in every life. So, Mother Nature concealed the past and kept the mind clean. However, some talents or tendencies from the past lives and will be there to make you an extraordinary scientist, physician, musician, singer or an actor or golfer, etc. Mostly people are born genius.

As per Vedanta, there is a law which governs life and death. This is the law of cause and effect that covers everything and the entire world runs under this law. The law of Karma is the law of cause and effect. As you sow, so shall you reap. Every effect must have a cause and vice versa. Something cannot come out of nothing. Existence cannot come out of nonexistence.

The doctrine of rebirth is a repercussion to the Law of Karma. The differences of personality that are found between one individual and another must be due to their respective past actions. Past action denotes past birth. Further, all your Karmas cannot certainly bear fruit in this life. Therefore, there must be another birth for enjoying the remaining actions. Each soul has a series of births and deaths. Births and deaths will continue until knowledge of the Immortal is attained. Very nicely expressed by Jalaluddin Rumi, a 13th-century Persian Sunni Muslim poet, Islamic scholar, theologian, and Sufi mystic, "I died as a mineral and became a plant, I died as a plant and rose to animal, I died as an animal and I was Man. Why should I fear? When was I less by dying?"

Good Karmas lead to incarnation into higher spheres and bad Karmas into lower. As long as Karmas—whether good or bad--are not exhausted, men do not attain the final liberation even in hundreds of births unless knowledge of the eternal is not complete. Both good and bad Karmas bind tight the *Atman* in their chains. Some are born with purity and extraordinary talents because they have undergone the various disciplines in their past lives. They are born as Avatar such as Jesus Christ, Shiva, Rama, Krishna, Buddha, and Guru Nanak Dev.

A newborn child manifests marks of joy, fear and grief. This is unconceivable unless we suppose that the child, perceiving certain things in this life, remembers the corresponding things of the past life. The things which used to excite joy, fear and grief in the past life, continue to do so in this life. The memory of the past shows the previous birth, as well as the existence of the soul. Michael Ondaatje, a Canadian novelist and poet, voiced on reincarnation, "For the first forty days a child is given dreams of previous lives. Journeys, winding paths, a hundred small lessons and then the past is erased."

Human beings do not come into the world in total forgetfulness and in utter darkness. They are born with certain memories and habits acquired in the previous births. Desires take their origin from previous experiences. We find that nobody is born without desire. Every being is born with some desires which are associated with the things enjoyed by him in the past life. The desires prove the existence of an individual soul in previous lives. Brian Weiss, an American psychiatrist, hypnotherapist, and celebrated author illustrated validity of reincarnation in his book, *Many lives and Many Masters*. His research includes reincarnation, past life regression, future life progression, and survival of the human soul after death.

The soul migrates with the astral body. This astral body is made up of nineteen principles, such as, five organs of action, five organs of knowledge, five *pranas* (breathing energy) mind, intellect, the subconscious mind, and egoism. This subtle body carries with it all sorts of memories, impressions, and lust, incomplete desires or affinities, of the individual soul. The subtle body moves towards heaven. When the fruits of good Karmas have been exhausted, it appears in a new physical form and reincarnates on this earth planet.

Those whose actions have been good are born in upright families, and those whose conduct has been evil are thrown into sinful wombs or lower births. This explains the disparities among human being.

The chains of desires tie us to this wheel of Maya or illusion, round of births, and deaths. As long as we desire objects of this world, we have to come back to this world in order to possess and enjoy them. But, when all our desires for the mundane objects cease, then the chains are broken and we are free and final liberation is attained.

If we unite ourselves with Him through meditation, good Karmas, and leave our desires, we will obtain immortality and eternal bliss. Bonds of Karma can be cut through knowledge of the Eternal that leads us to absolute bliss and peace. We will be freed from sins, passion, and the cycles of births and deaths.

Zeena Schreck, an American artist, musician, author, and the spiritual leader, remarked about the reincarnation of human consciousness, "Consciousness is endless, from one incarnation to the next. It simply will and does manifest in other places and times, regardless of what becomes of the human race."

Chapter Twelve:

Quantum Physics and Consciousness

"If you are'nt confused by quantum physics, then you haven't really understood it."

— *Niel Bohr*

During the past decades, physics and mysticism have been like two parallel lines which never converged due to their fundamental difference. Science believes in perception and wants to observe the reality where mysticism depends upon faith. Mystics perceive reality directly in its *Suchness*, *Is-ness*, *I-ness* or *That-ness*. However, during recent years, modern physics, and mysticism are trying to find a common ground through quantum physics or meta-quantum physics.

Consciousness may be defined as the experience of being awake and aware of the surroundings whereas the quantum physics is the study of the atom at subatomic level, at very small, nanosomic levels, beginning within nuclei, atoms and molecules. The laws that govern the behavior of the quantum mechanical system is fundamentally different than those which govern our macroscopic world of classical physics, comprising Newtonian laws. Classical concepts of time, length, and space do not flow in the quantum world.

Quantum Scientists believe that *quanta particles* are light particles of wave packets, comprising photons, quarks, leptons, electrons, protons, and neutrons which form atoms. These atoms form molecules and molecules form objects. These subatomic particles do not follow Newtonian laws of physics, thus making them more of a series of probabilities, rather than something scientifically defined and observed. Every visible thing is made up of invisible quanta particles. Moreover, in quantum physics, observing subatomic particles influences the physical processes taking place. Why does observation actually change the nature of what is being observed? Light waves act like particles and particles act like waves and the phenomenon is known as wave / particle duality. It has been proved by De Broglie's Equations. The formula shows how all matter has a wave/ particle duality, meaning that there are moments in which it behaves as a wave and other moments it behaves as a particle. Waves of particles under observation change their coarse to particles even when observed at the eleventh hours. Observation is consciousness. Does consciousness collapse the wave function? It is a matter of investigation. Dean Radin, parapsychologist and Senior Scientist at the Institute of Noetic Sciences, in Petaluma, California, conducted research on this concept. He conducted a pilot study comprising meditators against non-meditators in collapsing the quantum wave function. Data showed that consciousness affects the wave function. Results were more encouraging with the group of meditators. David Chalmers, philosopher and cognitive scientist at the New York University, also studied the effect of consciousness on wave function and revealed that consciousness changed the wave behavior.

Particles can go from one spot to another without moving through the intervening space, called *quantum entanglement*. Information moves instantly across immense distances. When two subatomic particles interact, they can get entangled which means their spin position or other properties become linked to a process unknown to modern sciences. Their communication travels faster than the speed of light. The affect can be millions of miles away. Albert Einstein called this as *"Spooky action of particles."* Subatomic particles behave in a very strange and unpredictable manner. In fact, in quantum mechanics the entire universe is actually a series of probabilities and do not follow any laws. No doubt, quantum physics is also known as a science of probability.

Light is the matrix of the quanta particles, atoms and molecules which keeps electrons tied to the nuclei of atoms, and atoms tied together to make molecules and objects. This can be compared with the Biblical belief of the creation of this world. First, the sound came. God said, "Let there be light," and there was light. Light was the essential force to bind particles together. Quantum physics also supports the Grand Unified Field of Energy which believes that everything in life is connected. When these quanta particles are generated within these particles exists pure energy which is not physically measurable but has its own intelligence. This purest form of energy is very subtle and named as *consciousness.* This is omnipresent, omnipotent, and omniscient. This exists everywhere, in the living and nonliving things. We human beings have our own separate and unique consciousness but it is also linked to the consciousness of the entire world. In brief, we are all connected. We are basically all one being, one consciousness, in many individual forms but differ due to our belief systems.

The concept that our consciousness seems to be made up out of quantized particles has been the subject of many mystical theories. Arthur Young, a great American inventor, physicist and philosopher thinks absolute spirit is a photon since its properties fits into the definition of soul. Photon has no charge, indivisible, beyond time, space and has the capability of creating matter. However, the French physicist Jean Charon, identified electron as the carrier of spirit. As per him there is a photon gas in the interior of an electron which can form structures and is a kind of inner memory of the electron. The consciousness of a man can be stored in electronic memory.

The German quantum physicist and mystic, Michael König, in the book, *Das Urwort* (*The physics of God*) mentioned the Firstword-theory. Our universe is an idea of God. All began with the wish of God that a cosmos with thinking beings should be there. He spoke a mantra (ELI - energy, love and information) and the multiverse was started. Consciousness is the center of the universe from which everything is developing. This enabled him to confirm through quantum physics, what was found by the enlightened ones and mystics of all time by the inner exploration of their consciousness. With his theory, he connects the traditional knowledge of the mystical philosophy with quantum physics.

Since electrons have an eternal life, Michael König developed in the 1980s the hypothesis that essence electrons form in the body of a man an eternal soul. They continue to exist after the death of the man and incarnate again later into a new body on the earth. In accordance with the traditional Indian philosophy, our entire universe exists out of three primary areas; the material cosmos, the afterworld and the heaven (God, Light World). Through spiritual practice, a person can develop a light body and ascend to higher realms of consciousness. On earth, there will be a golden age in the future, based on the association of spirituality and science. "And God's light will flood through all people, all love each other, they will laugh and be happy."

God is a higher dimension of consciousness consisting of energy, love and information (ELI) in the center of our multiverse. From this center, the Eta-particles (basic light-quantum) flow, form the afterworld and the material universe.

Recent discovery by a famous scientist, Robert Lanza, claims, that quantum theory proves consciousness moves to multiverse at death. According to Hindu Vedas astral body comprising the experience (consciousness) and memories leaves the human body after death and transmigrates to another body. The research of

Lanza confirms the five thousand years old Veda's concept of reincarnation.

Lanza's finding has stirred up many researchers who are interested in this field. This indicates that life does not end rather continues after death for ever. This gave birth to the new theory of biocentrism. Biocentrism means life and consciousness are fundamental to the universe. It is the consciousness that creates the material universe, not the other way around. This further confirms Max Planks statement that, "Consciousness is fundamental and matter is derived from it."

How does the human brain generate our subjective experiences? How does it manifest human consciousness? It is very difficult to explain where these subjective experiences come from. Moreover, how physics can explain this phenomenon. Some scientists feel that quantum physics can be used to explain the very existence of consciousness. Albert Einstein, Neils Bohr, Max Planck, and Schrodinger have worked on this subject. Lots of work has been done ranging from modern science to philosophy. Nothing conclusive is there and subjective experience could not be linked to any part of the human brain. Secondly, efforts to simulate the human consciousness with artificial intelligence have not brought any fruitful results.

Consciousness and quantum physics come together through the classical Copenhagen interpretation of quantum physics. It was developed by Neils Bohr and his colleagues at his Copenhagen Institute. In this interpretation of quantum physics, the quantum wave function collapses due to a conscious observer making a measurement of a physical system. This is the interpretation of quantum physics that sparked the Schrödinger's cat thought experiment in which a cat is both simultaneously alive and dead until someone looks inside the box that contains the cat. The two experiments reveal that reality revolves in the consciousness. If there is an observer the wave function collapsed. It is an astonished phenomenon, when you are observing electrons behave as particles and when you are not observing these behave like waves. That means reality is in our perception or consciousness. Albert Einstein was not very comfortable with observation theory. He said, "I believe moon is there, even when I am not looking at it." Again, it leads to the conception that reality is in our belief. Einstein was of course referring to the implications of the theory that the moon really is not anywhere until it is observed.

One version of the Copenhagen interpretation was proposed by John Archibald Wheeler and is called the Participatory Anthropic Principle (PAP). As per this principle, the universe requires observers because without the observers, the universe could not actually exit. The traditional Copenhagen interpretation requires an act of observation to resolve the superposition of states in quantum wave function. Any conceivable universe that does not contain conscious observers is obviously ruled out.

As per this interpretation, there must be an observer in place from the beginning of time and presence of God is essential, so that his act of observing the universe would bring it into being. Looks like we are again back to square one. *"Which came first, the observer or the particle?"*

The concept of using quantum physics to explain human consciousness got popular with Roger Penrose's book, *The Emperor's New Mind: Concerning Computers, Minds, and the Laws of Physics*. In this book, Penrose describes that the brain is far more sophisticated than the computer and the artificial intelligence. There are lots of variations in the biological system as compared to the static mechanical data depending upon programming. Artificial intelligence has created Robots which can perform many things including surgical operations. However, the human touch is still necessary. Moreover, it will be very difficult to incorporate emotions in the system. The book ultimately rests on the argument that the mind is more than the brain, which cannot be truly simulated within a conventional computer. As per Christof Koch, a neuroscientist and the Chief Scientific Officer at the Allen institute of neuroscience in Seattle, "No computer simulation, no matter how accurately it replicates a human mind, could ever become conscious. You can simulate weather in a computer, but it will never be *wet*."

Quantum physics is a science of probability and can never predict an outcome with certainty. If our consciousness is governed by quantum physical processes, then they are not deterministic, and we, therefore, have free will.

Modern quantum physics could not prove any of the spiritual realities. None of the founders of modern physics like David Bohm, Schrödinger, Heisenberg, and Einstein believed that the act of consciousness was responsible for creating particles at the quantum level.

Stuart Hameroff, Director, Center for Consciousness Studies, University of Arizona, Tucson, has done extensive research on Quantum Consciousness. His overview on the subject is as follows, "The general assumption in modern science and philosophy—the 'standard model'—is that consciousness emerges from complex computation among brain neurons, computation whose currency is seen as neuronal firings ('spikes') and synaptic transmissions, equated with binary 'bits' in digital computing. Consciousness is presumed to 'emerge' from complex neuronal computation, and to have arisen during biological as an adaptation of living systems, extrinsic to the makeup of the universe. On the other hand, spirituals, meditative traditions, some scientists, and philosophers consider consciousness to be intrinsic, 'woven into the fabric of the universe'. In these views, conscious precursors and Platonic forms preceded biology, existing all along in the fine scale structure of reality."

He further states, "My research involves a theory of consciousness which can bridge these two approaches, a theory developed over the past 20 years with eminent British physicist Roger Penrose. Called 'orchestrated objective reduction' ('Orch OR'), it suggests consciousness arises from quantum vibrations in protein polymers called microtubules inside the brain's neurons, vibrations which interfere, 'collapse' and resonate across scale, control neuronal firings, generate consciousness, and connect ultimately to 'deeper order' ripples in space-time geometry. Consciousness is more like music than computation."

No doubt, quantum physics is very popular today and trying to prove those latent concepts which used to be considered miracles of nature. However, by understanding quantum mechanics doesn't mean we are enlightened. Physics is obviously an indirect approach to reality, whereas meditation, or mystical disciplines are openly subjective approaches to reality. Each discipline reveals its own truth. The study of physics, as an indirect approach, like following a shadow will not get us enlightenment; and meditation, as a 1st-person discipline, will not disclose the location of a planet or an asteroid or an electron. The enlightenment is the realization of the unknown that is timeless, formless, omnipresent, and eternally unchanging. The content of physics is the understanding of the movement of form within time and space that is constantly changing. Moreover, if physics goes beyond shadows, it will lead to the metaphysical which has no form.

The two disciplines are very different and contradictory to each other. Therefore, it is concluded that quantum physics has not accepted the metaphysical concept of consciousness yet, though it is coming closer. Nevertheless, Quantum mechanics is mathematical descriptions and their practical implications are often sound unreasonable to a lay man.

James Jeans, an English physicist, astronomer and mathematician said, "We can never understand what events are, but limit ourselves to describing the pattern of events in mathematical terms; no other aim is possible. Physicists who are trying to understand nature may work in many different fields and by many different methods; one may dig, one may sow, one may reap. But the final harvest will be a sheaf of mathematical formulae. These will never describe nature itself. Thus, our studies can never put us into contact with reality."

Quantum physics suggests reality is simply a fabrication of our imagination. In the quantum world, we just cannot know anything with absolute conviction owing to a different set of rules. Even can't find the location of the particles due to wave like properties. It is quite evident, nature won't allow its fundamental elements to be boxed in.

What quantum physicists have recently discovered with modern technology regarding consciousness is not new. The sages, mystics, and enlightened masters of the past have preached it for eons, way before the technology existed. The quantum physicists reached to the same conclusion the ancestor sages and spiritualists had that "It is the energy from which everything came into existence."

"What quantum physics teaches us that everything
we thought was physical is not physical."
Bruce H. Lipton

Chapter Thirteen:

Consciousness and the Pineal Gland

"Keep the Pineal Gland operating and you will never grow old, you will be always young."

— Edgar Cayce

During recent years, the pineal gland has gained popularity in the scientific world. Scientists are trying to validate the relationship between the pineal gland and consciousness. Recently, the researchers at the University of Wisconsin, confirmed the presence of the DMT-synthesizing enzyme as well as activity of the gene responsible for the enzyme in the pineal gland. Later, University of Michigan demonstrated the presence of DMT in living rats. It was just like putting old wine in new bottle. Rick Strassman, Professor of Psychiatry at the University of New Mexico, has already established DMT as the spirit molecule in his book entitled, *DMT the Spirit Molecule,* a decade ago. Ample information is given on the psychedelic DMT and its formation in the pineal gland.

The pineal gland has been of great interest for thousands of years. Why all kinds of speculation, the mysticism, metaphysics, and philosophy are around this gland. Why is it known as a 'mysterious gland', 'stairway to heaven', 'throne of God' or 'tree of life'?

The function of Pineal gland in the human body was not clearly understood by medical sciences for some time. It remained a mystery for almost two thousand years in the west. Neurosurgeons and anatomists were inquisitive about the presence of this little solitary organ in the brain. Almost everything is symmetrical in the human body. Two eyes, two ears, two nostrils, two hands, two legs, two feet and even the brain has two sides. There is one area of brain that is not mirrored. This is the Pineal Gland. Although its connection to higher consciousness has been known to mystical and esoteric worlds for a long time, they considered it the interface between consciousness and matter. Almost all ancient cultures and religions have featured the pineal gland in their symbolism and iconography. The Sumerians, the Egyptians, the Babylonians, the Hindus, the Romans, the Greeks, the Buddhists, the Meson-Americans, the Catholic Church, and the Vatican have shown the symbol of the pine cone in one way or the other in their culture. The Vatican has even built an area within its grounds known as *Court of Pine* and is symbolized by a large statue of a pine cone (Figure 11).

Figure 11: Cone of Pine at Vatican Museum, Rome.

The ancient Egyptian believed the pineal to be the connection to universal *Realms of Thought*. The Egyptians adored this tiny gland and even preserved it separately during the process of mummification The founding fathers of American and Free Masons, added the all-seeing eyes (also known as "the Eye of Horus" from Egyptian mysticism), at the back of the dollar bill.

The symbol of the ancient pyramids on the Giza plateau in Egypt is also shown on the dollar bill along with a Latin motto *novus ordo seclorum*, a new order of the ages on the foundation of the unfinished pyramid. *Annuit Coeptis* is also written above the *all-seeing eye* meaning, Favors our undertakings. Who favors? The eye (Providence) does. *Providence favors our undertakings.* The significance of the Third eye is very spiritually described on the back of the dollar bill.

The pine cone on the top of Pope's staff signifies the importance of pineal gland. Likewise, Buddha's head is also shown in the pinecone shape.

Interest in the pineal gland was initiated in the seventeen century by a French philosopher and scientist, Rene Descartes (1596–1650). He proposed that the pineal gland the single organ of the brain, generated thoughts. He further emphasized this concept with his statement, "Cogito ergo sum" ("I think, therefore I am"). According to him we needed a source for thoughts. He further proposed that the pineal gland somehow was "the seat of soul", a connection between the soul and the body. How far is it true? So far, there is not a concrete explanation or evidence to prove this concept.

How close to the truth was Descartes? What was the basis of his statement? It will be very interesting to explore that. He had written two books on this subject, entitled *Treatise of Man* and *Passion of the Soul* illustrating the importance of the pineal gland.

In *Treatise of man*, Descartes described a conceptual model of man, namely creatures, created by God, which consist of two ingredients, a body and a soul. He mentioned, "These men will be composed, as we are, of a soul and a body. First, I must describe the body on its own; then the soul, again on its own; and finally, I must show how these two natures would have to be joined and united in order to constitute men who resemble us."

Descartes's explanation on the *seat of the soul* is, "My view is that this gland is the principal seat of the soul, and the place in which all our thoughts are formed. The reason I believe this is that I cannot find any part of the brain, except this, which is not double. Since we see only one thing with two eyes, and hear only one voice with two ears, and in short have never more than one thought at a time, it must necessarily be the case that the impressions which enter by the two eyes or by the two ears, and so on, unite with each other in some part of the body before being considered by the soul. Now, it is impossible to find any such place in the whole brain except this gland; moreover, it is situated in the most suitable possible place for this purpose, in the middle of all the concavities; and it is supported and surrounded by the little branches of the carotid arteries which bring the spirit into the brain."

The *Passions* of *the Soul* was a continuation of *Treatise of Man*. In *Treatise of man* he emphasized the body and wanted to focus on the soul later. The conclusion would probably have been that we are indistinguishable from the hypothetical 'men who resemble us' with which the *Treatise of Man* is concerned and that we are just such machines equipped with a rational soul ourselves. In the *Passions of the Soul*, Descartes started with man, a body and a soul.

Descartes's criterion for determining whether a function belongs to the body or soul was as follows: "Anything we experience as being in us, and which we see can also exist in wholly inanimate bodies, must be attributed only to our body. On the other hand, anything in us which we cannot conceive in any way as capable of belonging to a body must be attributed to our soul. Thus, because we have no conception of the body as thinking in any way at all, we have reason to believe that every kind of thought present in us belongs to the soul. And since we do not doubt that there are inanimate bodies which can move in as many different heat or more …, we must believe that all the heat and all the movements present in us, in so far as they do not depend on thought, belong solely to the body." Descartes work was interesting but inconclusive. He did not search beyond thoughts. Some researchers defended him but most of them rejected his theory.

The human body contains several endocrine glands such as the pituitary, pineal, hypothalamus, thyroid, parathyroid, adrenals, pancreas, and ovaries/testes. These glands secrete hormones which play significant roles in the development and growth of the body. Among them, pineal gland is the smallest endocrine gland, the size of a raisin (Figure 12).

The shape of the gland resembles a pine cone, that's why it is called pineal gland. It is located in between the two halves of the brain on the back portion of the third cerebral ventricle of the brain, which is filled with cerebrospinal fluid.

The clear, protein rich fluid provides cushioning for the brain. It also carries nutrients to and waste product away from the deep brain tissues.

The Human Brain

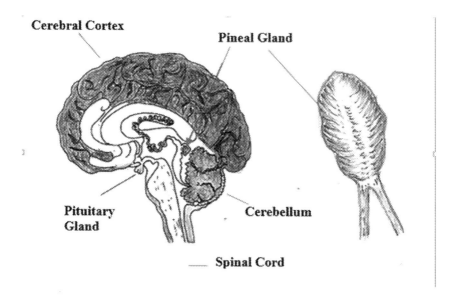

Figure 12: Location of the Pineal Gland in the Brain.

Since the pineal gland is located within the center of the brain just behind the eyes, it is linked directly to the sixth chakra point between the eyebrows, commonly known as the *third eye*. In terms of quantum science, Stephen Phillips stated in his book, *Extra-Sensory Perception of Quarks,* "The third eye's microscopic vision is actually capable of observing subatomic objects as small quarks. Thus, we can stimulate our pineal gland to achieve an awareness of things not perceived by our natural senses."

Ample amount of energy and blood flows through the pineal gland, as compared to the other glands in the human body. The location of the pineal gland close to cerebrospinal fluid channels and to the emotional and sensory brain center gives direct access to their properties. The sensory system is consisted of visual and auditory colliculi which are specialized brain tissues. They interpret and transmit visual and auditory impulses to the brain. Thus, the pineal gland is also known as the center of imagination and creation.

The very same rods and cones found within the eyes, can also be found within the composition of the pineal gland. The pinealocytes photoreceptor cells resemble the photoreceptor cells found in the eye. With this similar type of physiology, the pineal gland visualizes or imagines scenarios, fantasies, memories, and dreams. Pineal light sensitivity in humans relates to the opening of the third eye. Pineal gland is also known as *in the mind's eye*, or *the third eye* or *the sixth sense*. The Bible also mentioned the third eye, "If your eye be single your whole body shall be full of light." (Matthew 6:22).

The pineal gland is visible in the developing fetus at seven weeks or forty-nine days after conception. This is exactly the time when the differentiation of male and female is observed in the fetus. This co-relation is very interesting and needs further investigation.

The pinealocytes cells of the pineal gland secrete melatonin. Higher level of melatonin is found at an early age, which gradually decreases with ageing. Melatonin also helps regulate female reproductive hormones and sexual transformation. In addition to melatonin, serotonin is also produced by the pineal gland and it balances the mental state of mind. Dimethyl tryptamine (DMT) is also produced by the pineal gland. DMT also forms naturally at the moment of birth and death. It basically acts as a unique bridge between the world of living and the dead. It is a natural substance found in many plant species and is known for its psychedelic properties. DMT is produced naturally during the state of deep meditation in darkness. Dark meditation was in vogue in olden days. Most of the mystics of that time believed that if one continues to meditate in total darkness, he begins to observe inner energy in the form of light as the *third eye* becomes active. Meditation by Yogis and Rishis in the caves of Himalayas, India, is very well-known.

Melatonin and the Pineal Gland:

Melatonin is, *n-acetyl-5-methoxy-tryptamine*. It is the hormone of darkness. Day and artificial lights inhibit its production. Noradrenaline and adrenaline are two neurotransmitters (catechol amines) that turn on melatonin synthesis in the pineal gland. These neurotransmitters are released by the nerve cells nearly touching the pineal gland and attached to specialized receptors, and begin the chemical synthesis of melatonin. Pineal also secretes melatonin directly into the CSF (cerebrospinal fluid) where it can affect the brain more quickly. Disrupted levels of melatonin in the body can cause mood swings, depression, irregular circadian rhythms, and sleep disorders. Melatonin is also known as an anti-aging and anti-stress agent because it suppresses cortisol and is a powerful antioxidant. However, there is no scientific evidence to support these properties.

Melatonin and the Spirit Molecules:

Although the chemical structure of melatonin is pretty close to that of DMT, it is not psychedelic. So, melatonin is not the spirit molecule. However, pinoline and DMT, secreted by the pineal gland, are psychoactive, causing changes in perception, mood, consciousness, cognition, and behavior. Pinoline enables visions and dream states in the conscious mind and has been used by ancient Egyptians and Zoroastrians in their rituals.

The Pineal gland has the highest concentration of serotonin which is a precursor for pineal melatonin. Serotonin, melatonin, and tryptamine are converted to DMT by methyltransferase in the pineal gland. While methylation of methyl tryptamine twice, it forms Dimethyltryptamine. The pineal gland also produces *beta-carbolines* which inhibit the breakdown of DMT through monoamine oxidase (MAO). DMT is produced in the pineal gland during deep meditation, during birth, sexual ecstasy, extreme physical stress, and near-death experiences. It also changes our dream consciousness when it is released into the bloodstream during the Rapid Eye Movement

(REM) phase of sleep. DMT links the body and spirit because of its relationship to visionary experiences and non-ordinary states of transcendental consciousness. DMT is referred as the Spirit Molecule by Rick Strassman who has done significant work in this field. Pineal DMT production has cited some mystical or spiritual experiences such as near-death experiences, blinding white light, encounters with demons, angels, ecstatic emotions, timelessness, heavenly sounds, seeing heaven or hell, feelings of being dead and reborn, contacting the dead, and so on.

The pine cone shape with its spines and spirals, illustrates a perfect Fibonacci sequence—symbolizing growth and the unifying force that signifies creation, all comprise an activated pineal gland. In other words, the word pineal itself has the same root as pine-cone because the pineal gland exhibits a similar phyllotaxis pattern. The pattern is also known as the *flower of life* pattern. It is common in ancient art work depicted in enlightened or awakened beings. When the pinecone image is seen in sacred art work it represents the *third eye*. It represents the awakened *third eye,* single pointed consciousness directing the flow of evolutionary energy.

Pineal Gland and Health:

The pineal gland absorbs more fluoride than any other organ of the body. With aging, the pineal gland begins to calcify from the numerous substances found in our foods including soft drinks, processed foods, and fluoride in water, food and tooth paste. Recently, there has been a growing concern that electronic toys, cell phones, i-pad, computer Wi-Fi network routers are also harmful to the brain and the pineal gland.

It is very pertinent to find out the toxic effects of the chemicals and related substances used in our daily life. Approximately more than 60% of the USA water supply now contains sodium fluoride. The presence of sodium fluoride in food and vegetables causes additional problem to our health. A long term intake of sodium fluoride can cause cancer, thyroid problems, a low IQ, Alzheimer's disease and low melatonin formation and damage to teeth.

Preventive Measures:

First, protect calcification of the pineal glands by using less calcium supplements. Use calcium supplements of natural organic foods. Avoid the use of mercury during tooth fillings. Mercury is toxic to the pineal gland. Also avoid eating fish such as Tuna, dolphin fish, shrimp, and prawns. All these products have high concentration of mercury. Mercury can be eliminated from the body by eating green leafy chlorella, wheatgrass and spirulina. Use food and vegetables free from pesticides since these chemicals are toxic to pineal gland. Stop eating processed foods including artificial sugars. Drink fluoride free water and use fluoride free tooth paste. Certain vegetables are recommended to maintain a healthy pineal gland such as organic beets, garlic, seaweed, MSM, oregano oil, raw apple cider vinegar, and tamarind. Use of certain nutrients like vitamins K1 and K2 found in green leafy vegetables are very useful to pineal gland. The use of less electronics gadgets, performing yogic and breathing exercises regularly keep the pineal gland healthy.

Pineal Gland and Vibration:

Vibrations are the subtle potential factors of the universe of existence. All things are based on vibrations. In the early 1980s, the French musician Fabien Maman found that sounds can destroy cancer cells and invigorate healthy ones. It is a well- established concept that music affects our mood, memory, and physiology. Similarly, the pineal gland can also be activated through vibrations.

According to famous electric engineer Nikola Tesla, "Alpha waves in the human brain are between 6 and 8 hertz. The wave frequency of the human cavity resonates between 6 and 8 hertz. All biological systems operate in the same frequency range. The human brain's alpha waves function in this range and the electrical resonance of the earth is between 6 and 8 hertz. Thus, our entire biological system the brain, and the earth itself, work on the same frequencies. If we can control that resonate system electronically, we can directly control the entire system of humankind." Vibrations can purify the pineal gland, activate it, and raise consciousness. Matter, energy, and consciousness are interchangeable at different frequencies.

Magnetic Fields and the Pineal Gland:

The pineal gland is sensitive to all types of magnetic fields. The pineal gland's sensitivity to electromagnetic energy causes it to vibrate and activate in tandem with the heart. Synergistic effect of these two organs opens the third eye to a greater extent.

The gland is adversely affected by environmental electromagnetic radiation, too. Because of the pineal gland's connection with spatial orientation and circadian rhythms, our perception of space and time often shifts when the pineal is in a highly-aroused state.

Activation of the Pineal Gland:

1. Breathing: Various types of yoga breathing activate the pineal gland and ionize the flow of cerebrospinal fluid.

2. Tapping and messaging: Gently tapping and messaging the forehead between the eyebrows activates the pineal gland.

3. Chanting: Chanting mantras and singing any melodious song activate the pineal gland and energize the Cerebrospinal fluid.

4. Meditation: Regular meditation while concentrating on third eye also stimulate pineal gland.

5. Pressing: Pressing the tongue to the roof of the mouth activates the pituitary gland.

6. Squeezing: Squeezing the eyes, the muscular connection with the sphenoid activates the pituitary and pineal gland. Kegel exercise sends vibrations to the muscles that surround the pelvic floor. From the pelvis, the vibration then travels up the spine and to the occiput. The intracranial membrane system transfers the vibration to the center of the head, activating the pineal gland.

7. Spiraling: Spiraling movements in the Tai Chi symbol creates an electromagnetic field that energizes the CSF (cerebrospinal fluid) and enhances the power of the heart field, thereby activating the pineal gland.

8. Being in Darkness: Darkness stimulates production and release of melatonin, pinoline, and DMT. Meditation in darkness enhances the production of these chemicals.

9 Laughing and Smiling: Smiling opens both the heart and the crown, allowing more light to penetrate while also increasing the vibration of the organs. Laughing and smiling reduce stress and relax the body, which increases the flow of chi. Laughter also triggers the release of endorphins, promoting feelings of well-being. Relaxation increases blood flow, which amplifies the effects of the hormones released in the "Crystal Palace". Taoists call the center of the brain between the pineal and the pituitary "the Crystal Palace." (Thalamus, hypothalamus and anterior pituitary) and activates the pineal gland.

10. Focusing: Energy flows towards concentration. Thus, focusing on the "Crystal Palace" will activate the entire area including thalamus, hypothalamus, anterior pituitary and pineal gland.

11. Good diet and Hydration. To increase the activation of the pineal gland sufficient hydration is critical. If one weighs 200 lbs.,

50% of the body weight 100 oz. of water is required to maintain good hydration. Furthermore, a good, balanced diet is helpful comprising carbohydrates (50 %) proteins (20%) and fats (30%).

Conclusion: Very little progress had been made in the studies of the pineal gland in the scientific world until the second half of the nineteenth century. However, Descartes contribution revived interest in the pineal gland and melatonin was first isolated by Aaron B. Lerner in 1958. Melatonin was addressed as a *wonder drug* in the 1990s and then became one of the best-selling health supplements. The pineal gland research in the twentieth century has received some attention but did not make any significant progress. Later, Rick Strassman did interesting work on the pineal gland at the University of New Mexico. Despite the obstacles in his research, he remained quite dedicated to his search and published very impressive results. He designated the DMT as a *spirit molecule*. The out of body and near-death experiences and related hallucinations are all attributed to DMT psychedelic properties.

Descartes, proposed the pineal gland *as the seat of the soul*. A very charming and inquisitive expression he proposed, "There is a little gland in the brain in which the soul exercises its function in a more particular way than in the other parts." However, despite his extensive explanation in his publications, he could not come up with some scientific evidence in support of his statement. He could not establish any relationship or connection with the body and the soul except thoughts arise in the pineal gland. His explanation about the pineal gland being a solitary organ in the brain did not hold any ground. His statement could be based upon the 5000 years of spiritual concept of Egyptian or Hindus Vedas about the *third eye*. He thought he could scientifically prove it and would correlate soul and body connection through the pineal gland. Unfortunately, he could not do so. He stopped his inquiry at the level of thinking and did not go beyond thinking. Had he gone beyond thinking, he would have realized the concept of soul and its relationship to body. However,

Novalis, a German poet, author, mystic and philosopher of Early German Romanticism, said, "The seat of the soul is where the inner world and the outer world meet. Where they overlap, it is in every point of the overlap."

Until today, the concept of the pineal gland is based on pseudoscience and is connected to the *third eye*. The mysterious pineal gland is still a big challenge to scientists and researchers to unveil its mystery as *the seat of the soul*.

Chapter Fourteen:

Rightful Living To Raise Consciousness

"You are here to evolve and make your consciousness high. You are here to dance, sing and celebrate life. You are here to help others to make their life happy. We are here not to compete, but to learn, evolve and excel. We are not here to make divisions in the name of prophets and religions. We are here to encompass the world with love and light."

— *Amit Ray, Nonviolence: The Transforming Power*

There are very common inquiries I come across every day. What is the purpose of life? How should we spend our life? What is the right way of life? How we should raise our kids? How to expand our consciousness? It is very difficult to explain these things. There are many schools of thought depending upon the experience and success of an individual. My experience has been very different. I lived a life of discipline and infused the same to my off-spring. I never had any problem raising my kids. I rather enjoyed the period of their upbringing. However, the purpose of life is to spend right life sanctified with morals and ethics. Right life means to perform your duties with dedication and discipline. When you follow these disciplines, the consciousness is automatically raised. This can be achieved by following four disciplines as suggested by Shivpuri Baba who followed and preached these disciplines throughout his life. He died at the age of 138. He was in excellent health up to the last. He has few grey hairs even at the age of 113. He was a great mystic but not very well-known like Vivekananda, Swami Rama Krishna and Maharishi Raman. He kept a very low profile and lived a very simple and disciplined life in the forest of Nepal.

The sole purpose of human life is to find the Ultimate Truth, or God, and to this end a certain code of life is required—a spiritual, moral, and intellectual order. One should live a rightful life with a purpose and plan. The ultimate goal of life is to get rid of the cycle of life and death and obtain *Nirvana.* With rational attitude, positive thoughts and self-dedication, one can achieve his objectives. The key to success is to keep growing in all areas of life—physical, intellectual, moral as well as spiritual.

Physical
Intellectual
Moral
Spiritual

Physical:

The physical discipline falls into three categories. The first part is the care of the physical body. The second part is fulfilment of social obligations and the third part is to take care of professional duties to earn money with respect.

The physical body can be taken care of by controlling the five senses during the waking state of consciousness. Taking care of your eating, drinking, sleeping habits including sex. Perform daily exercise to keep your body healthy and in shape. Everything should be done in a moderate and balanced way. Excess of everything is bad. Keep your body healthy by controlling your anger, hunger and sleep. Eat simple foods. Control your emotions and speech. Think before you speak and look around before you leap. Observe cleanliness which is next to Godliness.

The next part is to realize your social obligations. Help the needy if you can. Perform your duty towards your community. Do good to others and forget. Do not expect anything from them. Expectations lead to frustration. Wish everyone good fortune and share their griefs and sorrows.

Perform your professional duties honestly. There are many ways to make money but the legal way is the best. Earn money with respect to maintain life and family. Look after your dependents and relatives. Do not fight with them for money and inheritance properties. Believe in "Sufficient unto the day is the evil thereof," (an aphorism which appears in the Sermon on the Mount in the Gospel of — Matthew 6:34). Its meaning is the philosophy that one should live in the present, without a care for tomorrow. Do not hoard money for generations to come. Life is very short, there should always be time for courtesy. Speak softly and gently. Avoid any harsh words to anybody. Without gratitude and appreciation, one can't be spiritual. Do not hurt anybody mentally or physically. Be calm and quiet. If speech is silver silence is gold. Do the necessary duties for maintaining life, and think mostly of God all the time.

Intellectual:

Intellectual discipline is to use your intellect wisely. Think positive, good thoughts give rise to good actions and repeated good actions will lead to good habits. Repeated good habits become the second nature of an individual which defines his or her character. Good and positive thoughts will give you a good moral character. The mind should be strong for good habits. Be fearless. Purity and stability of mind is required. Anger gives arise to delusion which causes confusion and loss of reasoning that leads to self-destruction.

Control your internal and external nature. Internal nature means anger, agitation, emotions, egoism, attachment, aversion, greed, and lust. The mind is capable of functioning with emotions as well as intellect in the right direction. A Person in whatsoever direction he may be, can uplift himself by his own efforts in the right direction by using his mind and intellect in the right manner. Each person is responsible for his or her own actions and should not blame others or God or fate. As per Buddha, "Since everything is a reflection of minds, everything can be changed by our minds."

External nature means do not react to external forces. If somebody tries to provoke you, and speaks harsh words to you or try to pick a fight with you, control your nature and do not react. Sometimes, it is better to swallow your pride or ego.

The mind is very active, unstable, and wanders widely and endlessly. Intellect is there to control the mind. The mind should stay under control. A weak mind indicates a weak soul that leads to poor will, the weak determination. Intellectual aspect is very important to decide between the right and wrong. An upright person is mentally equipoised, with controlled senses, truthfulness, renunciation, calmness, kindness. He should be humble, energetic, with purity of words, good deeds, and positive thoughts. Morihei Ueshiba, a martial artist and founder of the Japanese martial art of Aikido said, "Always keep your mind as bright and clear as the vast sky, the great ocean, and the highest peak, empty of all thoughts. Always keep your body filled with light and heat. Fill yourself with power of wisdom and enlightenment."

Moral:

Moral comes from the *Latin* word *moralitas* meaning manner and character. It is the icon to define right or wrong about our actions and thoughts and also to discern between good from bad. Moral values vary as per one's religion and culture. However, the sum of the core of all religions remains the same. As per Horace Mann, an American educational reformer, "Scientific truth is marvelous, but moral truth is divine and whoever breathes its air and walks by its light has found the lost paradise."

It is very pertinent for everyone who wants to live an upright life to follow a moral discipline to bear a good moral character. The start should be from the old scripters. Read religious and spiritual books like *the Bible, the Bhagavad Gita, the Upanishads, the Holly Vedas, the Puranas, the Koran*, and *the Dhammapada*. These should be followed according to your belief system. Study the lives and teachings of Buddha, Jesus, Mohammad and other spiritual personalities, such as Maharishi Raman, Rama, Krishna, Guru Nanak Dev, Mahavira, Swami Vivekananda, Swami Yogananda, Maharishi Mahesh, Shivpuri Baba, and Rajnish (Osho). All these realized souls direct to the path of self-realization, soul-realization, and God realization. All religions are like different rivers taking a different path but ultimately merged into the vast ocean of absolute consciousness. God is one, unknown, invisible, formless, unborn, immortal, omnipresent, omnipotent, and omniscient. God is above the religion. *Love is God. Nature is God.* If you want to love God, love his creation. The following are the suggestion for moral deeds.

Have compassion for all living entities. Do not hurt people, rather help them at the time of their need. Contribute at least 10 percent of your income to the needy people, educational institutions, students etc. Save 30 percent of your income to use that amount at the time of need. Be honest, and truthful. Avoid stealing, bickering, adultery, covetousness, anger, egoism, false pride, conceit, harshness, fear, finding fault with others, and blaming others,

Respect your parents. Your parents have not only brought you in this world but also groomed you to the best of their abilities and means. Their sacrifices are limitless. If you have difference of opinion with them, try to resolve with cool mind and respectful discussion. Be humble during the discussion. If you think you are right, try to convince them with respect. They have more experience than you. Listen to their advice very carefully. Do not walk away from them. Treat them and serve them with utmost respect. It is your duty to serve them in their old age as they have served you while bringing you up with utmost unconditional love. Their sacrifice is more than your services to them. Never make them feel that you are doing an obligation to them. One does not know the worth of water until the well is dry. You know their worth only when they are gone from this world. Then it is useless to cry. There is no point to hang their picture on the wall if you have not respected them while they were alive. One day you will be sailing in the same boat and your children will treat you the same way as you have treated your parents. What goes around comes around.

Be kind to children and old people. Raise your kids with the utmost care and be patient with them. Strive every day to be great parents so that your kids are better people when they grow and move out into the world on their own. Do not use any force or shout at them. Do not scare them, rather make them understand with love and affection. They have tender hearts and can be easily hurt. Do not compel them or force them to do anything which they do not like. If they have an aversion to certain foods, please do not force them to eat. If you forcibly get your task done, they may do so since they are too young to oppose you. But their helplessness accumulates hate in their mind for you which will create distance from you. They will never grow to an upright citizen. You will be responsible for inducing anger, hate and jealousy in them. Please raise your kids with high moral and ethical values. Help them to develop positive thoughts that will absolutely result into good actions, habits, and finally, excellent character. Encourage them towards sports and music. Try to understand their problems, spend time with them. Try to be their friend. Do not intimidate them.

To live happily with your partner is another challenge. Once you are married, it should be the union of two souls not two bodies. You should be happily married not just married. Marriage is an adjustment under one roof. Both the individuals are brought up in different environments, values and belief systems. The difference in their thinking and habits are obvious and imperative. Try to learn how to adjust and live under one roof with those differences. Make efforts to understand each other. Find a solution to remove your differences. Running away from each other would not change anything. If you do not have kids and you think that it was a misfit then better separate before having kids. Divorce is not the remedy, it is the last resort. There is no guarantee that the other person you choose is better or worse than the previous partner. Intolerance is the cause of divorces in present day and these are increasing day by day. Nevertheless, it is too hard on the children. To raise children by a single parent is very difficult financially, physically, mentally and spiritually. They can't do full justice in making them upright citizens. Adultery is another aspect of moral discipline which should be avoided. Most of the divorces are because of adultery, too.

Family values are another phase of good and healthy living. F.A.M.I.L.Y stands for *father and mother I love you.* Keep the family united and close. Family is the most important part of our life. No matter what we do we can always count on family. Differences in the family can be resolved with healthy discussions. Unresolved conflicts can create confusion, anger, hate, and ultimately bitterness in relationships. In the end, all you will ever have in life is your family. So, keep them close while you still have them around. Like branches on a tree our lives may grow in different directions, but our roots should stay as one. Prefer family and extended family over friends. Choose your friends wisely. They should have the same values as you possess. Sometimes, one can be in trouble in the wrong company. There is an old saying, a man is known by the company he keeps. Finally, do not ignore your neighbor, love *your neighbor as yourself,* though this concept is vanishing these days.

Do not be jealous with the progress of relatives and friends rather improve yourself to achieve your goal. Anger, resentment, and jealousy does not change the hearts of others, rather it will affect you. There will always be someone willing to hurt you, put you down, gossip about you, belittle your accomplishments and judge your soul. Just do not react and continue your efforts to achieve your dreams. You go on doing your good Karmas and do not worry about the results which are not in your hands. You can create your own destiny to some extent but you can only achieve whatever is in your fate. Things come and go at an appropriate time in your life. Most of the time, we do not have control over them.

Spiritual:

Buddha said, "Just as a candle cannot burn without fire, men cannot live without a spiritual life." Each discipline described above has a different field and different aim. With physical and intellectual disciplines, we achieve earthly happiness. It is world realization. Life will be happy and successful but death will end it. By controlling the mind, we conquer ourselves and achieve serenity and eternal bliss. It is soul realization. If we attach to soul-realization, it will also end with its existence. By spiritual discipline, we allow ourselves to be conquered by God. It is called God-realization which is objectively and absolutely required as the end and aim of existence. Spiritual discipline is beyond intellect and mind. There is no reasoning. No question asked about the existence of God or almighty or absolute consciousness. It is acquired by faith only. It is above the religion. Spiritual discipline means pertaining to the soul or spirit. Spirit comes from Latin *spiritus,* meaning breath. This reflects the belief that a person when born draws his first breath and dies drawing his last breath as the spirit leaves the body. Breath is considered *Prana,* a Sanskrit word, means life. The soul is the guiding intelligence, the evolutionary force and breath of life permeating the entire universe. Soul is the life force that transforms inert matter into living matter. Soul is the conscious intelligence that stirs the mind. The witness of the mind is soul (Atman). It witnesses the action and perceive of mind. Mistakenly believes that it is the doer or perceiver. Atman is not the seer. It is the witness of the seeing. Seer is mind and seen is the result of the senses.

So, *Atman* or soul is the focus for soul-realization which leads to God-realization. Soul realization leads to eternal bliss. Spiritual discipline can be obtained by meditation. Think of God alone and put away all other thoughts from our mind. When all else disappears, you will see the light in a flash. There are different ways of meditation. Choose any one. Intensify your longing for God. Let the thought of God alone be in your mind; destroy all other thoughts. God can be experienced, but can never be explained.

Meditate daily for 20 minutes, early morning, and late evening before going to bed. Meditate on Him, in the beginning with form and try to go beyond form. If you go on passing your time on meditating on God, God will come in a flash. If you see God or Truth, all your problems will be solved and no re-birth in the world. That means *Nirvana* or *Moksha* is achieved. After God realization, the soul immediately will not leave this body. It stays in the body so long as one enjoys the deeds of his present and past life.

The path of right living is very difficult and is comparatively easy to describe than followed. As they say, "An ounce of practice is better than tons of theory." If an individual followed and practiced these four disciplines, it would definitely lead to eternal bliss, self-realization, soul-realization and God-realization. The key to success is to keep growing in all areas of life disciplines, physical, intellectual, and spiritual.

Live in the now, the past is painful and the future is a fantasy. Connect to source by meditation. It is well expressed by Eckhart Tolle, an eminent author and spiritualist in his book, *The Power of Now: A Guide to Spiritual Enlightenment,* "If your mind carries a heavy burden of past, you will experience more of the same. The past perpetuates itself through lack of presence. The quality of your consciousness at this moment is what shapes the future." Get out of the acquired belief system. Unless you get out of the acquired belief system, you can't listen to yourself.

Raise your conscious level energy or frequency by being vegetarian. Get out of Ego. Living in Ego (LIE) is living with lies all the time. Stop judging and criticizing others. Do not react to the surroundings and controversies, take a neutral stand. Life is an Echo. What you send out, come back to you. What you sow, so shall you reap. What you give, so you get. What you see in others exists in you. Do not judge others—so you won't be judged. Radiate and give love and love will come back to you.

Control your thoughts, emotions and observations. Respect all life. Detach from attachments, it is illusion –Maya. Control your desire or completely get rid of them. Avoid the following: killing, sexual misconduct, lying, slander, abuse, idle gossips, malice, false views, and finally a *mindset that denies fundamental truths.* Believe in yourself. Listen to your inner voice. You have been programmed from the childhood with many beliefs and are not aware of your real identity or belief.

Buddha put it very nicely as "Believe not because some old manuscripts are produced, believe not because it is your national belief, and believe not because you have been made to believe from your childhood. But reason truth out and after you have analyzed it, then if you find it will be good to one and all. Believe it, live up to it, and help others live up to it."

> *"The purpose of life is to be free from suffering and to attain infinite bliss consciousness – and that is God,"*
> Paramahansa Yoganand

Chapter Fifteen:

The Quest For The Unkown

"The mind has always quest for the unknown."
Ravi K. Puri

U sually people are very inquisitive to find the unknown and ask various questions. The author has tried to explain them with some citation from the literature.

Q: Is there any destiny?

A: If God made man in his own image as said by Christ, then there is no destiny. We are all divine and are having human experiences over this planet. We can make our own destiny as said by Buddha. According to Hindu Vedas, Upanishad quotes about destiny as follow:

Watch your thoughts: they become words.
Watch your words: they become actions.
Watch your actions: they become habits.
Watch your habits: they become character.
Watch your character: for it becomes your destiny.
You are what your deep, driving desire is.
As your desire is, so is your will.
As your will is, so is your deed.
As your deed is, so is your destiny.

(As per the Brihadaranyaka Upanishad)

Ravi K. Puri, Ph.D.

Many great men believe that destiny can be created or altered by right thinking or by altering the attitudes of the mind. James Allen, a British philosophical writer known for his inspirational book, *As a Man Thinketh*, said, "You are today where your thoughts have brought you, you will be tomorrow where your thoughts take you." However, some philosophers, mystics and scientist believe in fate.

Somebody asked Maharishi Raman—"Are only the important events in a man's life such as his main occupation or profession, predetermined, or are trifling acts also, such as taking a cup of water or moving from one part of the room to another? He replied, "Everything is predetermined."

Albert Einstein not only agreed with Maharishi Raman, but went one step ahead of his belief. He said, "Everything is determined, the beginning as well as the end by forces over which we have no control. It is determined for insects as well as the stars. Human beings, vegetables, or cosmic dust. We all dance to a mysterious tune, intoned in the distance by an invisible power." It is really surprising to find this quote of Einstein.

As per Guru Nanak Dev, a renowned Indian mystic and Guru of Sikhs, "Every individual has born with his or her own destiny which depends upon his previous *Karmas*. One can change his destiny to some extent with his present *karmas* too."

When Osho, a great Indian mystic, was asked about destiny, he replied, "Consciousness is freedom. Man, is consciousness and cannot be slave. If man has a destiny then he is a slave. His life is predetermined." Osho built a 63,000-acre commune in Antelope, Oregon, in 1982. He had a dream of making it a utopian commune. He created his destiny but due to certain unavoidable circumstances, it did not last long. His paradise was lost in 1986. Maybe a Utopian Commune at Antelope was not in his fate. Fate is above destiny.

Q: What is the difference between fate and destiny?

A: These two terms are synonyms to each other in common discussion and usage but there is a significant difference between the two. Fate may be defined as, "The development of events beyond a person's control, as determined by a supernatural power. Fate is divinely planned, whereas destiny has the power to be influenced by man's actions."

One can create his own destiny as suggested by Buddha. One can plan and make efforts but the results of the efforts are in the hand of fate. Fate is above destiny. Destiny can be created only with the blessings of fate. Some people work hard honestly and plan their destiny but are not successful because of ill-fate.

Q: Is there any free will?

A: It is a very controversial question. The answer cannot be straight forward. There is no free will. If there is, it is all circumstantial. We never came to this planet of our own will, neither have we chosen our parents, relations, country and our environments. Our name and gender were not a free will either. We could not play with the toys of our choice during childhood and could not pick our nursery school. During childhood, we cannot eat foods of our choice. Our thoughts, emotions, impulses all are preceded by events in our life. There is always a cause for picking or choosing anything in life. Our actions have all sorts of invisible causes, desires and belief systems that occur in our brain. We decide any action owing to those latent factors and think we have a free will but in reality, it is not free. If you dig deep enough, you would see that there are factors that rule out those options as well as every other option. Change the belief system, you will get some other option. So free will depends upon these latent factors and it is circumstantial. Swami Vivekananda, said, "The will is not free--it is a phenomenon bound by cause and effect—but there is something behind the will which is free."

Q: What is God?

A: God is beyond human understanding and conception. He is impersonal, indefinable and incommunicable. He is omnipresent, omnibenevolent, omnipotent, infallible and omniscient. He is the past, present, and the future. He will continue to exist even when there is nothing in the universe. He cannot be confined to space and time. It is difficult to establish the presence of God. This unknown power controls the universe. He is unborn. He is fearless, shapeless and nameless and self-illuminous. He has no gender. *Then, what is He?*

He is such a mystery that all philosophers, mystics, and scientists have been trying to solve and understand him since time immemorial. He is a pure consciousness in the form of energy. Energy is neither created nor destroyed. This unknown energy controls the universe. This energy is absolute consciousness without any beginning and end. This is the only truth so far.

Q: Where can I find God?

A: God is within. Do not seek him outside. You do not have to go anywhere in the mountains or jungles. When we live daily with the conscious companionship of the supreme soul, then only our inner Divine Consciousness awakened. He is omnipresent, omniscient and omnipotent. Everything is within. You do not have to search for Him anywhere. He is in you and your existence is the way to him. You have come full of him. As per Teilhard de Chardin, the French idealist philosopher, "You are not a human being, having a spiritual experience. You are a spiritual being having a human experience."

Q: Where does God live?

A: God resides in nature. God is in every creature whether visible or invisible. He is in the living and nonliving.

"God sleeps in the rock
Dreams in the plants
Stirs in the animals
Awakens in man"
—Sufi Ibn Al 'Arabi

Q: What does He do?

A: He is in bliss all the time. He has given consciousness in the form of light to every living being. How a person makes use of that in the right direction, it all depends upon him.

Q: Who is the God of the Universe?

A: You are the one. The God is within you, there is no need to search him outside. The absolute 'I' is God within, nothing else. God is in the state of permanent bliss. *Sat chit Anand.* 'And I am Brahma', *Aham Bramsi.* Get back to your real self. Identify yourself with consciousness and when you do, the world will disappear. No object or duality any more, only subject, non-duality or self remains.

Q: Are we killing God every day?

A: If everyone is having God within him then why are people killing each other for the sake of religion? Killing any human beings ultimately is killing God. Consciousness is within every living organism in the form of the super power of God. In human beings, it is in the advanced stage rather more developed as compared to all other species. Killing a human being with enhanced consciousness, means killing God every day. Nevertheless, killing based on religion while pleasing their chosen God, is not the rightful act. Any religion is a belief-system, a faith, a discipline created by human being. For God, all religions are equal. God is above the religion. Love His creation then only you can love him.

Q: Is God aware of our thoughts, good and bad deeds?
A: Of course, He is. He knows everything all the time because He is you.

Q: Where do I come from?
Nobody knows that. Every honorable person wants to know his or her origin or permanent home. We have not come from anywhere. Everything is here. It is a transformation of energy from one form to the other. You can't come here by your will or leave by your will. Everything is predestined. Being born with a human body itself is destiny. You are a helpless being. He runs the show. Hold fast to Him and flow in the river of life. Human birth is the rarest of all births. Try to know the purpose of your life. There is no birth or death. Everything goes on changing form in the stream of eternity.

Q: Why am I here?
A: You are here to gain experience of human life. God has sent you for some purpose. You have come here to play your role in His play. Play your role whatever profession you choose to the best of your ability and honesty. Every bit of work is worship. Perform your daily activities called Karma. Action and reaction in mind lead to activities. Do not worry for its fruit. Do the work with attachment but without any desire to the results. Each soul is divine. So, treat your body as a temple and keep it pure. Avoid drugs and alcohol. Always remember Him who is inside the body in your sorrows and pleasure. Surrender to His Almighty and move according to Mother Nature. Life is a Struggle for existence. Do not be dependable. Try to survive on your own. Do not be a parasite. Work intelligently and diligently. Rationalize your faith and act. Do not be a blind follower of any belief system, follow your own instinct. You are born with mind, senses, desires, and attachments and have to fulfill them and use them to your best ability. You are a swirling vortex of limitless

potential who is here to shake things up and create something that the universe has never seen.

Q: When I die where will I go?

Very interesting and mysterious question that everybody wants to know. You do not go anywhere. Life is eternal and has no death. Death is nothing but transformation. Soul is going to transform and you are born again. When we give up the body, the ethereal body with all its memories goes away in the universe. After that it is a question of time, may be one day, may be a few years you come back in a different body. The cycle continues until you attain Moksha. Existence or life is energy. Energy is neither created nor destroyed but transformed from one phase to the other.

Q: What should I do in life?

A: Live in the present. Do not worry about the past and future. The past good or bad is painful and the future is fantasy. Nobody knows what is going to happen tomorrow. Perform your work honestly. Work is worship. Have patience with the vicissitudes of life which are gifted from him. Love your life, work, duty, colleagues, your neighbors, your coworkers, and do not hate your boss. Love your family and extended family; love everyone in your surroundings. Love all His creation. Keep Him in your mind while doing all your activities.

Q: What is the passage of the soul between death and birth?

A: It is an interval between the present state and the next state of life. After death, the soul migrates with the astral body in quantum state to the other world. This astral body is made up of nineteen principles; and five organs of action, five organs of knowledge, five breaths, plus mind, intellect, the subconscious mind, and egoism. This subtle body carries with it all sorts of impressions, and desires or tendencies, of the individual soul. The subtle body moves towards heaven. When the fruits of good Karmas have been exhausted, it gathers for itself a new physical body and reincarnates on this earth plane. Those whose conduct has been good attain good births and those whose conduct has been evil are thrown into sinful wombs or lower births.

Q: Who is the creator of the world?

A: There is not any creator of the world at all. All of this is a natural creation. If there is a creator, who created Him. There must be another creator who created Him…. Thus, there would be no end to this. They say, there is no beginning and no end, so there is no creator. If there is a beginning, there must be a creator. If there is no beginning then there is no creator. This world is without a beginning and without an end.

Q: What are we?

A: We are not a concept or object because we are what is aware of all concepts and objects. Therefore, we are Awareness. Because the body, and the world are objects, they appear in us—We do not appear in them. We do not appear in the body so we are not contained or restricted by it. We are eternal beings, without beginning and without end. We are gods within God, finite spirits within the Infinite Spirit. But what is 'spirit'? Yoga tells us that spirit is *consciousness*, hence we are eternal consciousness, each of us eternally individual and distinct.

Q: Who is the doer?

A: Nature is the Doer, whereas Atman is Non-Doer. It is a wrong notion that I am doing. According to some mystics' nature is the inherent characteristics complex that makes a person do things. There is not an independent doer of anything. We are only instruments. That is further clarified –It goes through planning.

The only place in the doer ship is the thought. You are the planner. All that materializes in front of us in this life, is the outcome of planning in the past life through inner intuition (deep inner intent). In other words, all the present events of one's life are the effects of the cause created in the past life. The present actions will create the future of an individual soul.

Things just happen. Sometimes, we work very hard and the result is negative and we are disappointed. We blame the fate or destiny or Almighty for that. We even console ourselves by saying, "Everything happens for a reason." The other times we do not make much effort, everything goes smooth and we are happy and take the credit of being the doers. Certain things are circumstantial depending upon many factors. We are like a gyro or puppets and strings are not in our hands. The winding string is the cause and spinning is the effect. We dance according to the tunes of the circumstances, you may call it nature. When the man realizes, he is neither the doer nor the enjoyer, the ripples of his mind are stilled.

Q: How to separate 'I' from 'My'?

A: 'My' and 'I' are the two parallel lines. They run together in life, but always remain separate. Once the 'I' is separated from 'My', self-realization occurs. One has to drop off all the 'My' from the 'I'. 'I' is Atman (soul) and 'My' is all Maya-illusion. One gets attached to 'My'. 'I' gets attached to 'My'. 'My' is the temporary state where as 'I' is the permanent state. 'I' is the only independent form. The real 'I' has no possession. 'My' has all the possessions. 'My' mind, my body, my wife, my beloved, my brother, my car, my house and so on. 'I' is self and 'My' is no self. 'My' is a separate identity from the self. The body can be 'My'. 'I' is real whereas 'My' is relative to 'I'. 'My' is not real and separate from 'I', and it is all Maya-illusion. I am totally separate from everything that is mine. Once you acquire this knowledge of the real 'I', everything is accomplished. When 'I' is detached from the 'My' everything becomes crystal clear.

Whatever is left, is your real self. You are free. No attachment, no hate, no possession, no ego, no greed, and no lust. The real 'I' has no possession.

Q: What is the difference between consciousness and mind?

A: The mind is a modified consciousness. The human mind is restless. It tends to go out and reach out to things and objects it likes. It withdraws and moves away from things it dislikes. Consciousness is inert, unchangeable. It is like a mirror that reflects images of the mind without losing its quality.

Q: What is mind, intellect and soul?

A: The mind is restless like a monkey. Intellect is comparatively calm and has the tendency to evaluate, reason out and judge things, events and situations it encounters using such means as analysis, comparison and imagination. It reacts to situations either positively or negatively. We must now understand mind and soul. The mind reacts quickly, the soul does not. The mind attaches to materialistic objects, the soul does not. The soul remains inert and witnesses the activities of the mind and intellect.

Q: What is the difference between ego-self and real self?

A: The ego-self is dynamic and active. The real self is the passive witnessing soul. It lives only for a time in its entirety. It is eternal, unborn, and immortal.

Ego-self is outgoing and dispersive. Real self is self-absorbed and self-contained. Ego-self interacts with sense organs. Real self does not interact. It is absolute. Ego-self interacts with the object and accumulates Knowledge. The residual self is formed out of the ego-self goes with the soul to the next birth and becomes the seed for the next Ego-self. Ego-self cannot be transformed to real self even after purification and transformation.

Q: Is brain and mind the same?

A: No, they are not. The brain is comprised of proteins, fat and cholesterol molecules. It is formed of neurons. It is matter. How come a nonmatter mind can be produced by a matter? The brain is just like a TV and cannot operate without electricity. Electricity is pure mind or consciousness. The scientific community has spent enormous amounts of time and money studying the brain. They believe that the brain controls everything and the mind is a function of the brain. In fact, the mind is a bundle of thoughts created by consciousness. Consciousness works through the brain but does not require a brain to exist.

The mind is unmanifested and metaphysical and does not live in the brain. The mind can pass through the smallest cell in one's body or can travel into the future or across thousands of miles of empty space. The mind can heal incurable diseases. Through telepathy the mind can travel thousands of miles away and can make contact to the desired person.

Neuroscientists and brain researchers could not study the mind even with cutting edge technology such as ultra microscopy, X-Ray, MRI or a CAT scan whereas brain activity can be studied.

Q: Can physics explain consciousness?

"Physics cannot prove even physics. How can it prove consciousness?" said Eugene Wagner, a Hungarian-American theoretical physicist, engineer and mathematician. He further added that it was not possible to formulate the laws of quantum theory in a fairly consistent way without reference to consciousness.

Q: **What is the difference between duality and non-duality?**

A: In duality the mind is restless, full of thoughts. Duality means living in two phases in the world such as good or bad, happiness or sorrow, joy or pain, wet or dry, black or white, dark or light, start or stop, hell or heaven, etc., all beginnings or endings happen in duality because of time and space. There is a subject and the object in duality. When you are looking at a beautiful rose flower, there is a subject (you) and the object (flower). Duality gives birth to divisions, sufferings, illness, illusion, fear, rejection, and abandonment.

In non-duality, there is neither a knower (subject) nor a known (object) because they have become one. The flower and you have become one, the moment you are absorbed in its beauty. That moment is bliss. It is complete. Omniscience is self-completion. No further desire and anticipation since there is no time and space in this phase. Each moment is total and complete within itself. There is no past, present or future. There is total bliss and stillness. During this phase, the mind is still without any thought.

Q: **Does meditation and orgasm create the same effect on the brain?**

A. It is a very interesting topic. Spiritual teachers have been contemplating this topic for years, but research shows that orgasm and meditation create the same effect in our brains. According to a recent article in *Scientific American*, both meditation and orgasm decrease our sense of self-awareness says author Nadia Webb, a neuropsychologist from New Orleans. Studies observed that when the brain is in action, the right hemisphere lights up during orgasm and left hemisphere remain silent. In fact, on the contrary, the left is most active when recalling happy memories. All emotions occur here.

However, a new concept is developing. Bliss, both sacred and profane, share the reduction of self-awareness, alterations in bodily perception and decreased sense of pain. Pleasure is also linked to a loss of awareness of the boundaries of our body, and this, too, involves both sides of the brain. Orgasm and meditation dissolve the sense of physical boundary, but the activation patterns are distinct. Meditation does so in a somewhat cerebral way, altering bodily self-awareness by enhancing activity in specific brain regions.

But during orgasm, the cerebellar deep nuclei and vermis, also in the cerebellum, glow. Unlike meditation, orgasm seems a heightened sense of being within one's body rather than the sense of being outside of it. In other words, both experiences lead to a temporary stoppage in the incessant flow of our internal commentary and there is an altered state of consciousness for a brief time. Though orgasm is only momentary but it gives a pure joy and solace to the couple if their bodies and souls vibrate with the same frequency.

Osho, the Indian mystic formerly known as Rajneesh, was famous for his views about the mystical value of an orgasm. He has written a couple of books on this topic: *From Sex to Super-consciousness,* and *From Lust to Lord.* As per him, "The experience of orgasm itself is always nonsexual. Even though you have achieved it through sex, it itself has no sexuality in it, my own understanding is that meditation has grown out of the experience of orgasm." He further explained that during the moments of climax of mind, the mind becomes empty of thoughts. All thoughts drained out at this moment, and this emptiness of mind, this void, this vacuum, this freezing of mind, is the cause of the shower of divine joy. He was ahead of his time and misunderstood by people 25 years ago. Now a majority of people are accepting his concept and taking credit for that. It is well said; a prophet is seldom recognized during his lifetime.

Still, orgasm is no replacement for meditation. Meditation and orgasm light up various parts of the brain. Meditation, studies have shown, lights up the left prefrontal cortex — an area associated with joy and happiness. But during an orgasm, the left cortex remains totally silent. Meditation has also been known to create lasting change in the brain through a thickening of the cortex. In gist, both the techniques, meditation and orgasm are important in life to keep the balance of the body, brain and mind. Also, both hemispheres of the brain remain active.

Q: What is the difference between a concept and reality?

A. A concept is a thought of a separate object together with a name or identifier of the object. Thoughts begin to arise in early childhood. Thoughts means duality. The infant's mind contains few concepts whereas the sage's mind sometimes may contain many thoughts but the sage always sees directly that separation is an illusion. He believes in non-duality. Without thoughts, there are no objects (e.g., in dreamless sleep, under anesthesia, or in Samadhi) because, by definition, an object is the thought of it. Reality is not a thought. Rather, it is the absence of separation that leads to non-duality.

Q: What is the 'I'-Object?

A. When an 'I'-concept is believed to be separated from Awareness, it is said to exist as 'I'-object. However, in reality, there is no 'I'-object. We are not objects and we do not exist as objects. We are Reality (Awareness).

Q: What is the difference between self and self-less?

A: 'I' is self and 'My' is self-less.

Q: What is the personal sense of doer-ship?

Along with the illusory 'I'-object, arises also the sense of personal doer ship. However, since there is no 'I'-object, there is no doer, no thinker, no chooser, and no observer. Therefore, we have no control. Thus, whatever happens, happens. Whatever doesn't happen, doesn't happen.

Q: What is awakening?

A. Awakening is enlightenment. It is your true nature. Enlightenment is understanding your true self. Your true nature is your pure mind. Pure mind is stillness. Stillness is timeless. Timeless is eternal. So, you are the peace of stillness. It leads to the realization that I am not separate from Him and I have never been separated. We are all connected and love His creation. Awakening carries with it the realization that I am not the doer. Awakening is the awareness that Reality, which is what I am, has never been affected by any concepts. Awakening is the awareness that my true nature is to do unconditional love. Hate, anger, ego, jealousy, and discrimination should not have any place in life.

Q: What can we do to awaken?

Try to find your true nature. Who am I? Your pure mind is your true nature. Pure mind is stillness. Attain stillness by purifying your mind. Since direct seeing shows that there is no doer, there is nothing that the individual can do to awaken. Since awakening transcends time, no practice that occurs in time can bring about awakening. Thus, most practices do not bring about awakening. However, direct seeing can bring about awakening because direct seeing is timeless seeing. Still your mind, stillness is timeless and eternal.

Q: What is awareness, consciousness and mind?

A: Awareness is your being. Presence of that which is aware of itself. Awareness is the only one who knows itself. Awareness means consciousness plus being. Consciousness is your being and the dust (in the form of thoughts) that awareness collects around it, is your mind.

Q: Explain karma, cause and effect?

"To every action there is an equal and opposite reaction," Newton's third law of nature applies here. The world is like a pond where every stone thrown causes ripples among millions of other ripples. When we pursue our own self-interest, we are adding to a sea of selfish behavior in which we too live. Sooner or later, the consequences of our actions come back to us. Whatever we sow, so shall we reap.

Karma or actions are the impressions stored in the mind in the form of personality—accumulation of everything we have done and said and thought. Our actions, right or wrong follow us wherever we go. "Fly in the sky and burrow in the earth, we cannot escape the consequences of our action." says the Buddha. We can run but cannot hide. All of us have karmic scores to settle, a book of debits and credits that is constantly growing. If we could not clear these accounts in this life. We have to come back in physical form as per our karmas that remained to be worked out.

Q: Is consciousness localized in the brain?
It is not localized in the brain. It is metaphysical as per Vedanta philosophy. Scientists have not been able to find any suitable answer though they are trying to explore this riddle through quantum physics. Their initial finding is that consciousness is localized in the neurons.

Q: Is sex an altered state of consciousness?
Yes. This is true. But it is only possible if there is a deeper connection with your partner. Neuroscientist Adam Safron of Northwestern University explains, "Sex is a source of pleasurable sensations and emotional connection, but beyond that, it's actually an *altered state of consciousness.*"

In an article published in *Socio-affective Neuroscience & Psychology*, Victoria Klimaj and Adam Safron investigate the mystery of the orgasm. The concept that sexual experiences can be like trance states is in some ways ancient which is being supported by modern understandings of neuroscience. Tantric meditation had been used in India since time immemorial and is similar to this idea.

Q: Which gives more pleasure, sex or meditation?

A: Sex is a temporary pleasure and energy is being dissipated during the process. Energy is being wasted and causes physical weakness. One lives a life of non-understanding awareness. Sex cannot be sacramental unless both the partners vibrate with the same frequency. Moreover, sex always depends upon the partner. His or her involvement or proper tuning is very important even for the temporary pleasure. However, there is no guarantee, one gets pleasure or frustration after the performance. Further, the sex energy is focused on the object and going outward. Sex is a physical pleasure. Sensual pleasure does not last long. That does not mean we should give up sex altogether, in fact with this understanding, we can make sex sacramental.

Meditation accumulates energy and pleasure both. Energy falls back to being, moves inward. Energy becomes illuminous, turns into awareness, and gives ecstasy, ultimately leading to permanent bliss. Meditation creates the total orgasmic phenomenon without any dependence on anybody else. Further, it is a continuing inner source of energy, independent, and full of ecstasy. The more one meditates, the more he gains physically, mentally and spiritually. Meditation is divine and gives inner pleasure and satisfaction. Divine pleasure leads to everlasting bliss. It is very nicely expressed by Abhijit Naskar, a celebrated author and neuroscientist, in his book, *Love, God & Neurons: Memoir of a scientist who found himself by getting lost,* "Just like love becomes consummated upon the attainment of orgasm, all the faith and divinity in the world reach their ultimate existential potential upon the attainment of Absolute Unitary Qualia or simply Absolute Godliness."

Q. What had happened before the big bang?

A. There was no time before the big bang. So, no information is available.

Q: What is time?

A. Time is the perception of duration of change. Where there is a sequence of events, there is time.

Q: What is space?

A: Where there is an extension, there is a space.

Q: When will time end?

Time requires consciousness. If there is an observer, time exists. If there is no observer, there is no time. Time is the perception of duration of change. If there is no change, there is no time. Time started with the beginning of the universe 13.7 billion years back. It will end with the universe.

Q. What is the expanding universe expanding into?

A. We are part of the universe so how do we know what is happening outside. It is like asking a fish the expansion of the ocean.

Q: Why am I born?

A: It is very difficult to answer this question. I am sure there is not any scientific explanation to this question either. However, according to Vedanta, your desire brings you in this world. Until your desire is fulfilled, you will continue your birth. Once your desires are fulfilled, then you will be free from the cycle of birth and death. Desires will bring you back again and again in this world. Buddha also emphasized the concept of desire and stated that desire is the root cause of all sufferings. If you want to get rid of your miseries, get rid of your desires.

Q: What does happen after Death?

A: Of late, quantum physics is exploring this aspect but the findings are inconclusive. As per Vedic Philosophy, energy is transferred again depending upon your desire and you are born again. Your past desires steer you in that direction and you are born again. Your present is dependent upon your past life and your future on your present actions. So, a person is born again depending upon his past karmas and latent desires. The cycles of birth and death will continue until the human soul achieves Moksha or Nirvana.

Chapter Sixteen:

Consciousness: The Ultimate Reality

"That which appears, and disappears, is not real."
Ravi Puri

The quest to know and understand the ultimate reality is as old as humanity itself. Philosophers have debated about existence and the origins of reality for thousands of years. Religions also tried to explain in their own ways, forms and faiths. Science has been struggling to find the ultimate reality and could not come to any conclusive explanation. Will science discover the ultimate reality? Can religion be able to prove it?

The concept of Reality here means, the quest to find the truth about existence. First of all, we need to discern myth from reality. Myth means a traditional or legendary story dealing with supernatural beings. All religions have 'creation myths' but they are usually not true. Reality means having verifiable existence. Something existed, exists, or will exist. If something neither appears nor disappears, existing all the time is known as Real. Consciousness fits into this definition. Consciousness is reality not myth. Either nothing is consciousness or consciousness is inherent in all things. Everything exists in consciousness, living or nonliving. All objects appear in consciousness. All stars, galaxies, nebulae, planets, and universe are part of consciousness. The very appearance of life and consciousness means that both must have been present in latent form even before the Big Bang.

As per Samuel Butler a British novelist, "In the higher consciousness there is still unconsciousness, in the lowest unconsciousness, there is still consciousness. If there is no consciousness, there is no thing, or nothing. To understand perfectly would be to cease to understand at all."

Consciousness knows itself, through itself, for itself and by itself. Everything is consciousness. It remains unchanged. It is omnipresent, omnipotent and omniscient. It is immortal. In essence, it is **"OM,"** the first primordial word. It is neither created nor destroyed. It remains the same. It is metaphysical. It is invisible and has no beginning and no end. It is all pervasive. It has no shape and no name. No gender and no age. It is pure emptiness. There is only one space in the universe empty space that is consciousness. All these criteria fit into the definition of divinity. So, 'I'- consciousness is divine and real. Nothing functions without consciousness. Beyond consciousness, there is infinite. It is limitless. Your denial of consciousness is also in consciousness. It is very well articulated by Siri Aurobindo Ghose, a celebrated Indian yogi, poet and spiritual reformer, "Consciousness is the fundamental thing in existence. It is the energy, the motion, the movement of consciousness that creates the Universe and all that is in it. The microcosm and the macrocosm are nothing but consciousness arranging itself."

Further, consciousness is just like a mirror or screen which remains the same but reflects the images. Lots of movies can be projected on the screen. You can see them but the screen is unaffected. The screen is only real whereas the movies are not. If there is a rain or fire or floods depicted on the screen, in real sense screen is not affected. The screen remains the same. Everything is an illusion except the screen.

Likewise, place daffodils before the mirror it will reflect daffodils. Now replace daffodils with lilies, it will now reflect lilies. Place any object and see the reflection of that object. The mirror is clean and has its quality intact. Similarly, consciousness is crystal clear and not changed but gets modified in the human body as per thoughts. The mind is modified consciousness. It is like two banks of a river—consciousness and modified consciousness. Modifications of existence or consciousness give rise to relative existence. Relative knowledge gives rise to relative consciousness not absolute consciousness. The mind is a collection of thoughts and thinking process. In the absence of thoughts there is no mind. Pure mind in reality is consciousness but it is overpowered by the senses of the body and becomes modified consciousness. The mind is sentient but appears to be insentient. A pure and uncontaminated mind is absolute consciousness. The mind is 'I' that clings to past, present and future. The mind is duality, whereas consciousness is infinite 'I', and nondual. The absence of thoughts means the absence of modification. To think of things experienced and not experienced is also thoughts. Your consciousness is the ability to experience the matter and non-matter through your senses. What has not come to your experience does not exist. In short, our thoughts create our reality. Our thoughts are according to our belief system. Hence, in order to change our modified consciousness, we need to change our belief system. Albert Einstein put it as, "The world we have created is a product of our thinking; it cannot be changed without changing our thinking. If we want to change the world we have to change our thinking...no problem can be solved from the same consciousness that created it. We must learn to see the world a new."

We have the power to change simply by the way we think. It has been proved scientifically that we create the structure of our neurons via thoughts. Neurons send the signal to hypothalamus which starts manufacturing victim peptides. Accumulation of the victim peptides results in pain in the body. The more the cells of our body receive victim peptides, the more they get addicted to them. By thinking painful thoughts, we are producing more victim peptides and cycle continues. Soon a person is sinking down into depression and feels terrible—mentally, emotionally and physically. On the other hand, if a person thinks positive and brings unconditional love and good feelings in his life, he can reverse the entire process by right thinking. This clearly reveals that we can create our own reality. The power is *within* not *without*. Jesus Christ eloquently stated, "The Kingdom of God is within you" (Luke 17:21).

Consciousness is the fundamental reality at the basis of all creation. As per the Indian Vedas: "That from which the whole phenomenal universe has come into existence, in which it exists, and into which it returns at the time of dissolution, know that as the Reality, that is your True Self or Consciousness."

Consciousness is the ultimate reality. This reality has no beginning and no end; we may call it consciousness or existence that runs the universe apart from our own efforts. There is only one reality, one endless source of energy called absolute consciousness. It is infinite, immortal and beyond time and space. Physicists are also trying to believe that consciousness is not a byproduct of anything but itself the ultimate cause. Glen Peter Kezwer, scientist, meditator and author believed, "Consciousness is not subject to the structures of quantum rules because it is neither physical matter, nor is it restricted to time and space".

Erwin Schrodinger, a celebrated physicist and Nobel Laureate felt the same way, "Vedanta teaches that consciousness is singular, all happenings are played out in one universal consciousness and there is no multiplicity of selves." He also emphasized that, "The unity and continuity of Vedanta are reflected in the units and continuity of wave mechanics."

We are all connected to one the Grand Unified Field of Energy. Quantum scientists are now supporting the theory of The Grand Unified Field. It is very nicely expressed in Upanishad as well:

"As by knowing one piece of gold, dear one,
We come to know all things made out of gold-
That they differ only in name and form,
While the stuff of which all are made is gold
So through that spiritual wisdom, dear one,
We come to know that all life is one."
(Chandogya upanishad vi.1.5)

Further, science keeps on dissecting, the physical universe searching for answers through the quarks, leptons and photons whereas the spiritual world understands that the physical universe is the outcome of the nonphysical universe which is the Grand Unified Ocean of Consciousness. One cannot find answers to reality by searching the byproducts of reality. One must seek the answers in the cause of reality.

Salutations to quantum physicists and astrophysicists who are finally moving towards spirituality and verifying many things that spiritual traditions have always known and preached. However, there are so many questions (listed below) which are still unknown, and the modern sciences are struggling to find their reality. So far, these questions are an unsolved reality. It is hoped that these questions may have some suitable answers in the near future.

- *How did consciousness arise?*
- *What is the source of consciousness?*
- *Can we simulate Consciousness?*
- *Can consciousness be transferred from one person to another one?*
- *Can we upload consciousness to a computer?*

- *How did the Big Bang occur? Where did it occur in the universe? What existed before the Big Bang? Is it accurate to explain the Big Bang with cosmic inflation?*
- *Where is the center of the Universe?*
- *Why is there more observable matter than the antimatter in the universe? What is the future of the universe? What created the universe? Why is the expansion of the universe accelerating?*
- *Are there multiple dimensions?*
- *Why do we have the unseen effect?*
- *What is the origin of Mass?*
- *What is the nature of the arrow of Time?*
- *What is the nature of dark matter and energy which comprises 96 percent of the universe? What is the nature of dark matter?*
- *Why are we unable to perceive more than 99 percent of the electromagnetic spectrum of light, sound and other energies that make up the reality?*

Afterword

It was not easy for me to write this book. Many a times, I thought to leave this task unfinished since ample information was found available on this subject during the survey of the literature. However, these findings also revealed equal numbers of controversies on the topic. So, it was thought, desirable, to continue the present topic. The book comprises my modest effort in a very simple and primitive form to throw some light on consciousness as the ultimate reality. This reality has no beginning and no end; we may call it consciousness or existence that runs the universe apart from our own efforts. We are all connected but behave differently due to our belief systems and ego-selves. My inquisitiveness about the absolute consciousness increased day by day during the process of completing the book. Many of my dogmas were changed and I felt transformed physically, mentally, and spiritually. The feelings are ineffable. I sincerely hope my effort may be useful to the readers of the book.

—Ravi K. Puri
Columbia, MO 65203
USA

Bibliography

Ammon-Wexler, J., "Pineal Gland and Your Third Eye: Develop Your Higher Self," Quantum Self Group, Inc., Standpoint, Idaho, USA, 2013.

Baars, BJ., "On Consciousness," Bernard J. Baars Publisher, San Diego, CA, 2011.

Bennett, JG., "Long Pilgrimage- The life and Teaching of Siri Govindananda Bharti, known as the Shivpuri Baba," Hodder and Stoughton Ltd, London, UK,1965.

Bucke, RM., "Cosmic Consciousness, A Study in the Evolution of the Human Mind," Published by MCMI, Digital Edition,1901.

Cordea, SG., "Quantum Consciousness: The Road to Reality," AuthorHouse, Bloomington, Indiana, USA, 2011.

Cruttendent, W., "Lost Star of Myth and Time," St. Lynn's Press, Pittsburgh, PA, 2006.

Debroy, B., and Debroy, D., "The Holy Vedas," B.R. Publishing Corporation, 12th Edition. Delhi, India, 2011.

Dimitrov, T., "50 Nobel Laureates, and Other Great Scientist Who Believe in God," USA, e-book, 2008.

Dunn, J., "Consciousness and Absolute-The Final Talks of Sri Nisargadatta Maharaj," Acorn Press, Durham, NC, 2004.

Easwarn, E., "The Dhammapada, Nilgiri Press, The Blue Mountain Center of Meditation, second edition. CA, 2011

Falk, GD., "The Science of the Soul on Consciousness and the Structure of Reality," Blue Dolphin Publishing, Inc., Nevada City, CA, 2004.

Giri, SY., "The Holly Science," Self-realization Fellowship, LA, 1894, Edition, 1977.

Haisch, B., "The God Theory- Universes, Zero-Point Field and What's Behind it All," Weiser Books, San Francisco, CA, 2009.

Hawkins, DR., "The Eye of The I," Veritas Publishing, Arizona, USA, 2001.

Hawkins, DR., "Power Vs Force," The Hidden Determinants of Human Behavior, Hay House Inc., CA, USA, 2002.

Jaynes, J., "The Origin of Consciousness in the Breaking down of the Bicameral Mind," Houghton Mifflin Company, Boston, NY, 1982.

Kansal, A., "The Evolution of Gods," HarperCollins Publisher, India, 2012.

Kezwer, GP., "Meditation Oneness and Physics-A Journey through the Laboratories of Physics and Meditation," Sterling Publishers Pvt. Ltd, New Delhi, India, 1995.

Lanza, R., and Berman, B., "Biocentrism," Benbella Books Inc., Dallas, Texas, 2010.

Linetsky, BL., "Free Will: Sam Harris Has it (Wrong)" Cognitive Consulting Inc., NY, 2013.

Maarten, AS., "Divine Living: The Essential Guide to Your True Destiny," Indigo House, South Africa, 2012.

Martin Birrittella, M., "Field of Love: Without This Thought …Who AM I"? Delhi International Press Library, USA, 2013.

Naskar, A., "Love, God & Neurons: Memoir of a Scientist Who Found Himself by Getting Lost," An Amazon Publishing Company, USA, 2016.

Neuron, AO., "Quantum Metaphysics: Consciousness, Space-time, Life, Your Reality, and the Mysteries of the Universe Explained," Qmetaphysics.com., 2016.

Osho, R., "From Sex to Super Consciousness," Rebel Publishing House Gmbh, Cologne, West Germany,1980.

Osho, R., "Awareness, The Key to Living in Balance," St Martin's Griffin, NY, 2001.

Parnia, S, and Young, J. "Erasing Death, The Science that is rewriting the Boundaries between Life and Death," HarperCollins, NY, 2013.

Penrose, R., "The Emperor's New Mind: Concerning Computers, Minds, and the Laws of Physics," Oxford University Press, UK, 1989.

Phillips, SP., "Extra-Sensory Perception of Quarks," Theosophical Publishing House, Wheaton, Ill, USA, 1980.

Prasad, H., "Know Thyself: A Guide for Spiritual Aspirants," Yellow Bay Books, UK, Digital Edition, 2011.

Puff, R., "Spiritual Enlightenment: Awakening to the Supreme Reality," *eBookIt.com.*, 2011.

Ramachandran, VS., "The Tell-Tale Brain: A Neuroscientist's Quest for What Makes us Human," W.W. Norton Company, NY, 2011.

Ray, A., "Nonviolence: The Transforming Power," Inner Light Publishers, India, 2012.

Sam, H., "Free Will," Free Press, A Division of Simon & Schuster, Inc., NY, 2012.

Schultes, R., and Hofmann A., "Plants of the Gods—Origins of Hallucinogenic Use." McGraw Hill Book Company, NY, 1979.

Strassman, R., "DMT: The Spirit Molecule, A Doctor's Revolutionary Research into Biology of Near-Death and Mystical Experiences." Park Street Press, Rochester, Vermont, USA, 2001.

Subramanyan, SV., "Gain Wisdom- Maharishi Patanjali Way," Pustak Mahal, New Delhi, India, 2010.

Susan, B., "Consciousness—A very Short Introduction," Oxford University Press, Oxford, NY, 2005.

Swami, A., "The Mystery of Death," Ramakrishna Vedanta Math, India, 1967.

Swami, A., "Body and Soil: An Integral Perspective"
Atma Books, 3rd Edition. USA, 2012.

Swami, P., "The Inner Consciousness How to Awaken and Direct it," The Vedanta Society of San Francisco, San Francisco, CA,1921.

Swami, S., "What Becomes of the Soul After Death," The Divine Life Society, UP, India,1972.

Swami, V., "The Yoga Sutra of Patanjali —The Essential Yoga Texts for Spiritual Enlightenment," Watkin Publishing, London, 2007.

Tomkins, P., and Bird, C., "The Secret Life of Plants: a Fascinating Account of the Physical, Emotional, and Spiritual Relations Between Plants and Man." Harper & Row Publishers, Inc., NY, 1973.

Toll, E., "The Power of Now," Namaste Publishing and New World Library, Novato, CA,1999.

Vilayanur, SR., "The Tell-Tale Brain, A Neuroscientist's Quest for What Makes Us Human," W. W. Norton Company, NY, 2011.

Walters, JD., "Awaken to Super-consciousness-How to use Meditation for Inner Peace, Intuitive Guidance, and creative Awareness." Crystal Clarity Publishers, Nevada City, CA, 2000.

Weiss, BL., "Many Lives, Many Masters" Simons & Schuster, NY, 1988.

Wilber, K., "Quantum Questions, Mystical Writings of the World Greatest Physicists," Shambhala Publishers, Inc., Boston, Massachusetts, 2001.

Yogananda, P., "Autobiography of a Yogi," Self-Realization Fellowship, LA, CA,1946.

Glossary of Terms

Advaita: Nondualism, one ultimate reality.

Ahamkara: Egoistic, arrogant, proud

Atman: Soul

Avatar: Descendent of God

Beingness: Condition of having existence

Brahma: The supreme power, God as creator

Buddha: Awakened one, a title for one who has attained enlightenment.

Dawaper Yuga: Bronz Age, Era

Dhammpada: Sacred book of the Buddhists

Divine Years: 12,000 divine years is equal to 4 Yugas (4,320,000 human years). 24,000 divine years = 12,000 revolution of Sun around its dual.

Ego-cons: Ego consciousness composed of mind, intellect, body and consciousness

Kal Yuga: Iron age, Era

Karmas: Actions

Kuran: Sacred book of The Muslims

Lepton: A lepton is an elementary, half-integer spin (spin/2) particle that does not undergo strong interactions. Two main classes of leptons exist: charged leptons, also known as the electron-like leptons, and neutral leptons (better known as neutrinos).

Maya: Illusion

Moksha: To get rid of the cycles of birth and death

Musk: Perfume use as fixative

Neti, Neti: Not this not that

Nirvana: Extinction of selfish desire and selfish conditioning

Quarks: is an elementary particle and a fundamental constituent of matter. Quarks combine to form composite particles called hadrons, the most stable of which are protons and neutrons, the components of atomic nuclei.

Samsara: Wheel of existence, individual soul returns again and again to know various forms of embodiment.

Prana: Life, pertaining to breath. There are 5 types of pranas. Vyana (diffusion-pertaining to nervous system) udana (ascending-throat, upper chest) Prana (inward moving-heart, chest lungs) Samana (equalizing-naval-digestion) and Apana (below the naval-excretory and reproduction).

Purana: Sacred text of Hindus

Sanskaras: A deep mental impressions produced by past experiences

Satya Yuga: Era, Golden period

Tattva Brahma Assi: I am Brahma

Treta Yuga: Era, Silver Age

Upanishads: Upanishads are the Bible of Indians. There are 108 survived. Age of the Upanishad is unknown.

Vedanta: Philosophy of Vedas

Vedas: Holy literature of Hindus. There are four Vedas. Sam Veda, Yajur Veda, Athar Veda, and Rig Veda

Yoga: Union between the human soul and divine essence.

Printed in the United States
By Bookmasters